W9-APK-857

MOG

METROPOLITAN OPERA GUILD
COMPOSER SERIES

WAGNER

the Man and his Music

JOHN CULSHAW

Picture Editor: Gerald Fitzgerald

E. P. DUTTON
in association with
METROPOLITAN OPERA GUILD
New York

The illustrations in this book were made possible through the kindness and help of many generous people. The picture editor expresses deep appreciation to Alison Ames, Huguette Ancandau (Paris), Herbert Barth (Bayreuth), M. Todd Cooke, Manfred Eger (Bayreuth), John W. Freeman, Alfred F. Hubay, Robert Jacobson, Maria Jeritza, Lotte Lehmann, Scott Mampe, Anita S. Morceri, Francis Robinson, Dorle Soria, Robert A. Tuggle, Ann Viles, Stephen Wadsworth, Friedelind Wagner and L. Wenzel (Leipzig).

Copyright © 1978 by The Metropolitan Opera Guild | All rights reserved | Printed in the U.S.A. | No part of this publication may be reproduced or transmitted in any form or by any means, electronic or mechanical, including photocopy, recording or any information storage and retrieval system now known or to be invented, without permission in writing from the publisher, except by a reviewer who wishes to quote brief passages in connection with a review written for inclusion in a magazine, newspaper or broadcast. |
For information contact: E.P. Dutton, 2 Park Avenue, New York, N.Y. 10016 | Library of Congress Cataloging in Publication Data | Culshaw, John | Wagner, the man and his music | (The Metropolitan Opera Guild composer series) Includes index | 1. Wagner, Richard, 1813-1883. I. Series: Metropolitan Opera Guild. The Metropolitan Opera Guild Composer series | ML410.W1C9   782.1'092'4   78-842 | ISBN: 0-525-22960-4 | Published simultaneously in Canada by Clarke, Irwin & Company Limited, Toronto and Vancouver | Picture Editor and Captions by Gerald Fitzgerald | Project Coordinator, Leslie Carola | Production Director, David Zable | Text set by Pyramid Composition Company, Inc. | Display type set by Expertype | Designed by The Etheredges | 10 9 8 7 6 5 4 3 2 1 | First Edition

CONTENTS

FOREWORD

THE Metropolitan Opera Guild Composer Series is an introduction to the lives of major composers whose works form the backbone of the opera repertory. Though designed for the general public, these brief, authoritative, illustrated books are a valuable addition to the library of every music-lover.

The authors are well-known authorities whose names are familiar to a nationwide public through association with the Saturday afternoon intermission broadcasts from the Metropolitan Opera.

Photographs and documentation have been selected by Gerald Fitzgerald, associate editor of *Opera News,* the magazine of the Metropolitan Opera Guild, and editor of the annual Guild calendars from which many of the illustrations are drawn. The stories of the operas were compiled by Stephen Wadsworth.

The series was conceived by Dario Soria, managing director of the Metropolitan Opera Guild, and planned in conjunction with Leslie Carola of the Guild and the editors of E. P. Dutton.

THE PUBLISHERS

ACKNOWLEDGMENTS

THE problem of writing a very short life of Wagner is obviously that of deciding what to include and exclude. I am deeply grateful to Gordon Parry for the help he has given me in research and in sifting the mountainous material, and to Richard Wagner's grandson, Wolfgang Wagner, for verification or comment on certain doubtful issues.

The standard work of reference remains Ernest Newman's *Life of Richard Wagner* (4 volumes, New York, Knopf). A substantial one-volume biography is Robert W. Gutman's *Richard Wagner: The Man, his Mind and his Music* (New York, Harcourt Brace). Gutman's *selected* bibliography lists over three hundred sources, which gives but a glimpse of the material available to those who may wish to investigate far beyond the bounds of my essay.

JOHN CULSHAW

London 1977

PICTURE CREDITS

BETH BERGMAN (*New York*): 41(r), 61(l), 116, 117 (top) · THE BETTMANN ARCHIVE (*New York*): 140(r) · BIBLIOTECA NAZIONALE MARCIANA (*Venice*): 136-37(center) · BISCHOF AND BROGL (*Nuremberg*): 77 · BURRELL COLLECTION: 11, 29(Johanna Wagner) · ANTHONY CRICKMAY (*London*): 115 · CULVER PICTURES, INC. (*New York*): 31(r), 38(Nordica) · ERIKA DAVIDSON (*New York*): 142(l) · DEUTSCHE GRAMMOPHON (*New York*): 61(r) · DEUTSCHE PRESSE AGENTUR (*Nuremberg*): 35(top) · FRANK DUNAND (*New York*): 58, 59, 95(r), 99, 108-109, 112, 117(bottom), 132-133 · GÜNTHER ENGLERT: 142(r) · HEINZ EYAELL: 125(r) · WALTER GRILL (*Munich*): 147 · HARVARD THEATER COLLECTION (*Cambridge*): 97(r), 105(top 1) · DMITRI KESSEL (*Paris*): 84, 120 · DMITRI KESSEL/TIME-LIFE PICTURE AGENCY (*New York*): 37(theater), 47, 50(Mathilde Wesendonk) (From Time-Life Records Special Edition: *Richard Wagner, the Man, his Mind and his Music* © Time Inc.) · SIEGFRIED LAUTERWASSER (*Uberlingen-Bodensee*): 43, 63, 78-79(top), 81, 94-95(top), 118(bottom), 122(r), 130(l), 131, 143, 144-145 · HARVEY LLOYD (*New York*): 135, 148 · LOUVRE (*Paris*): back cover portrait · WERNER LÜTHY (*Basel*): 15(bottom) · METROPOLITAN MUSEUM OF ART (*New York*): 52 · METROPOLITAN OPERA ARCHIVES (*New York*): 26, 69(r), 129(r) · MUSEO TEATRALE ALLA SCALA (*Milan*): 25(r) · WERNER NEUMEISTER (*Munich*): front cover portrait, 45, 147 · GREG PETERSON (*San Francisco*): 22 · ERIO PICCAGLIANI (*Milan*): 21(top r, bottom), 113 · WILHELM RAUB (*Bayreuth*): 15(top), 35(bottom), 111, 118(top) · EDUARD RENNER (*Frankfurt*): 130(r) · SAN FRANCISCO OPERA: 22, 56 · FRANZ SCHNEIDER (*Lucern*): 87(Triebschen) · DONALD SOUTHERN (*London*): 94-95(bottom) · STAATLISCHE SCHLÖSSER, GARTEN UND SEEN (*Munich*): 44 · MICHEL SZABO (*Paris*): 101 · THEATER-MUSEUM (*Munich*): 8(drawing), 19(Tichatschek, Kriete), 55(playbill), 69(l), 82 · WIST THORPE (*New York*): 32-33 · ROBERT A. TUGGLE (*New York*): 30(r), 31(l), 41(top 1), 73 · FRIEDELIND WAGNER (*Cleveland, England*): 141 · RICHARD WAGNER ARCHIV (*Bayreuth*): 92(bottom), 139(bottom) · RICHARD WAGNER GEDENKSTÄTTE (*Bayreuth*): ii, 2, 7, 12, 13, 16, 30(l), 48, 49, 50(Otto Wesendonk), 66, 74(Hanslick), 78-79(bottom), 87(Wagner), 88, 89, 92(top), 102(l), 105(bottom 1, r), 110(r), 122(l), 124-125(top and bottom), 127(group), 134, 136(l), 137(r), 139(top), 140(l)

WAGNER

I

ACTIVITY WITHOUT REWARD

THERE is only one word to describe Wagner: he was a man possessed. Yet by itself that word is not enough, for in all ages there have been those whose driving force has led them misguidedly to create the unwanted. The result is what might be called the artistic litter of the centuries, and what we can learn from it is that the urge to create is not always the province of genius. In a way that is how Wagner started. He was no prodigy, but the urge to express himself in words and music was so powerful that it took him years to bring his genius under control. At the age of thirteen he began an epic prose tragedy called *Leubald und Adelaïde*. By the end of his nineteenth year, only four years after he had started any serious study of music, he had composed several overtures, a quantity of piano music, and a Symphony in C

"The Red and White Lion" (second building from the corner), an inn
in the Brühl, Leipzig's Jewish quarter, was the birthplace of
Richard Wagner. The composer's father, Carl Friedrich Wagner,
a lawyer with deep interest in the theater and many artist friends,
succumbed to typhus six months after his son's birth, May 22, 1813

major which he finished in six weeks. He started and abandoned an opera called *Die Hochzeit,* whereupon he promptly began the libretto of another called *Die Feen.* Little or none of this amounted to anything at all: there was no sign of the kind of innate genius displayed at the same age by the young Mozart or Schubert. Instead there was an abounding, irrepressible energy in both life and music, and the first signs of the ruthlessness which was to cause those who befriended him so much agony in later years.

It is hard to be charitable about Wagner the man. His incomplete autobiography *Mein Leben* tells only that part of the truth which he chose to reveal. His early biographers allowed themselves to be dazzled by the glare of his musical and dramatic genius, and so, under the scrutiny of Wagner's widow, selected their material carefully, omitting anything which might detract from his official image. Yet for much of his life he was in debt, which never prevented him from trying to adopt a lifestyle he could not possibly afford; he was arrogant; he dabbled in everything from radical politics to Buddhism, anti-Semitism and vegetarianism; his hatred of those who opposed him was boundless, but at least it can be said that they knew where they stood, which scarcely applied to those who befriended him since he had no hesitation in abandoning them once they had served his purpose. Physically, he was a small man with a very large head, and much given to vanity. He did not just *like* the good things in life: he *demanded and needed* them. In the early years they were mostly beyond his reach, but once he was in a position to get what he wanted his requirements were all but insatiable.

All this (and indeed a great deal more) may be difficult to excuse though not to explain. It took Wagner more than half of his lifetime to come to terms with his genius, but that struggle and the consequent outpouring of his mature works took an absolute precedence over everything else. Modesty was not in his nature, for he had nothing to be modest about. The sheer industry of his work is hard to comprehend. It is not just the size and scope of his dramas and the fact that he wrote the words as well as the music that causes amazement: it is that he also found time for prose of considerable (some would say inordinate) length; he read his own poems aloud at countless private gatherings; he conducted and toured; and toward the end he supervised the design, building and administration of his own theater in Bayreuth, Northern Bavaria. Everything he did became news, subject on the one hand to mockery and caricature and to fanatical veneration on the other. But, when all else has been said, the fact remains that he changed the language of music in a way and with an effect that has no parallel in history. Even today research into his life is still not complete, and controversy still rages over the alleged political, social and ethical implications of his work. Yet of one thing we can be certain, which is that no other figure in musical history ever exerted such an influence *outside* the field of music.

We have reason to be less certain about the identity of his father. His mother, Johanna Wagner, gave birth to Wilhelm Richard—who never used the Wilhelm part of his name—in Leipzig on May 22, 1813. She was herself the illegitimate daughter of Prince Constantine of Weimar, who had secretly cared for her education until she married Friedrich Wagner, a police actuary whose passion was the theater. Friedrich was the father of eight of her surviving children, if we count Richard as one of them; and from the records of the baptismal ceremony held in St. Thomas' Church on August 6 it is clear that Friedrich accepted Richard as his son. The doubt concerns their family friend Ludwig Geyer who, having started life as a law student, became for a while a portrait painter and then turned to the stage. When he was in Leipzig he stayed with the Wagners and his relationship with Johanna was particularly close.

It is only worth dwelling upon the doubts about Richard's parentage because, much later in life, he himself seemed, if somewhat obliquely, to share such doubts. Friedrich Wagner's theatrical interests in Leipzig included a number of actresses; it seems unlikely that his wife was unaware of them and even less likely, in view of subsequent events, that Ludwig Geyer would lose the opportunity to console her to whatever extent she would permit. So much is surmise; but what is not is that Richard's baptism was inexplicably delayed for two and a half months (whereas his elder brother had been baptized within five days of birth), and that during those months Johanna made a perilous journey of a hundred and fifty miles across country ravaged by war in order to stay with Geyer in a hotel at the resort of Teplitz, where the Leipzig theatrical company had moved for the summer season. It is almost certain that she took the infant Richard with her, leaving Friedrich to tend the others; but why should she have done so, if not to show Richard to his real father, Ludwig Geyer (who had not been in Leipzig at the time of the birth), and to consult him about the future? It would also explain the delay in the baptism, and why the dangerous journey was kept a secret for more than a hundred years.

Friedrich Wagner died of typhus in November 1813, when Richard was six months old. In August 1814 Johanna married Ludwig Geyer, and a daughter, Cäcilie, was born to them six months later. She was therefore almost certainly Richard's sister rather than his half sister, and she became his inseparable companion in childhood. Fifty-five years later Cäcilie sent Richard copies of letters which Johanna and Geyer had written to each other in days gone by, and Richard's affectionate if typically evasive reply adds further weight to the theory that not only was Geyer his father, but that Richard eventually knew that he was.

One month after Geyer married Johanna the family moved to Dresden, where Geyer was employed by the Court theater. He was an

Wagner may have been the natural son of actor-playwright Ludwig Geyer (right in a self-portrait), who painted a likeness of Wagner's mother, Johanna Rosine (far right), while she was still the wife of his friend Carl Friedrich Wagner. Geyer later married this woman with nine children, herself the illegitimate daughter of Prince Constantine of Weimar

excellent father, and Richard worshipped him. (When Wagner was fifty-seven and preparing his autobiography *Mein Leben* he asked for the emblem of a *Geyer,* which in German means vulture, to decorate the title page. The gesture was affectionate, and has nothing to do with our image of the vulture as a repulsive bird of prey). But in 1821, when Richard was eight and a half, Ludwig Geyer died and the family ran into financial difficulties. Richard's eldest sister Rosalie acted at the Court theater and thus provided the most stable part of the income; the rest, such as it was, came from relatives and lodgers. Geyer's early death must have had a profound effect on Richard, for by his own admission he was a rebellious child who took badly to school discipline; nor did he reveal any artistic talents, unless we count that swashbuckling drama called *Leubald und Adelaïde,* which he began at the age of thirteen and which seemed to horrify his family.

In fact little of importance happened until the family moved back to Leipzig in 1827. Richard was then fourteen, and although he had taken his first piano lesson at eleven he had shown little interest in music. (It is worth mentioning, however, that Greek mythology had already attracted him, and so it can be said that there were early indications that he would become *some* kind of man of the theater. It ran in the family anyway. We know how much Friedrich Wagner loved the theater, and Ludwig Geyer was an actor; Richard's elder brother Albert and his sister Klara were both singers, and two other sisters were actresses.) The turning point came in January 1828, when Richard entered St. Nicholas' School in Leipzig and was suddenly exposed to Beethoven's symphonies and the *Egmont* music, and to Mozart's *Requiem* and Weber's *Der Frei-schütz.* With an urgency that was later to determine all the major decisions in his life he turned to music to the detriment of his other studies, except where they had some kind of musical or dramatic application. He began to study Shakespeare, Goethe, and Schiller; he heard *Fidelio* and

Wagner began work on his first completed opera when he was nineteen,
basing his three-act libretto on a fanciful play by Carlo Gozzi,
La Donna Serpente. To his dismay, he never heard the piece performed.
Not until June 29, 1888, five years after his death, did Die Feen
(The Fairies) reach the stage (left), at Munich's National Theater

immediately tried to write a soprano aria because he was overwhelmed by Wilhelmine Schröder-Devrient's performance as Leonora. By the time he was seventeen he had experimented with a piano sonata and a quartet; he was transcribing Beethoven's Ninth for piano, and towards the end of December 1830 his Overture in B flat was performed at the Leipzig theater. What was more significant than anything he wrote was the sheer application he brought to the task of writing. He may have been immature and headstrong, but he had no longer any doubt at all about the direction in which he was going. At the age of eighteen the youth who had discovered music only four years earlier entered the University of Leipzig to begin his serious studies.

We need not dwell on the university years, except to note that when he was not studying harmony and counterpoint with Theodor Weinlig (who was the Cantor at St. Thomas') he was experimenting with composition; and when he was not composing he was drinking, gambling, occasionally getting involved in duels—and borrowing money. During vacations he traveled widely whenever he could find a school friend willing to pay for the trip. When he was nineteen he made his first visit to Vienna and Prague, taking with him the C major Symphony he had written in six weeks. Students in Prague played it for him, but his mind was already turning toward the theater. He wrote the poem and the music for the opening scene of an opera to be called *Die Hochzeit (The Wedding)* which he then abandoned, only to start thinking of another based on Gozzi's "La donna serpente" which eventually became his first opera, *Die Feen (The Fairies)*. In 1833 there were three important events in his life: the C major Symphony was played at the Leipzig Gewandhaus and was well received by the critics and public; his brother Albert helped him to obtain the modest position of chorus master at Wurtzburg; and he completed *Die Feen*. But acceptance of *Die Feen* was continually postponed by the Leipzig theater, and in May of 1834 he set out on a visit to

Minna Planer, a gifted young actress of some beauty, entered Wagner's life in 1834, becoming his wife two years later. He was then working as a fledgling maestro in Magdeburg, where he conducted his first opera, Mozart's Don Giovannni. In the brief poem with self-caricature at far right, Wagner begs his bride's forgiveness for a trifling offense

Bohemia—again with a friend who was willing to pay for the journey. This time he was thinking of another opera to be called *Das Liebesverbot,* based on Shakespeare's *Measure for Measure.*

Die Feen was written very much in the style of Marschner and Weber; *Das Liebesverbot* was a deliberate attempt to court public success by writing an "unrestrictedly sensual" opera in the more popular style of Donizetti and Bellini, but without their economy of resources. The score is huge in size and duration, and only now and then is there a fleeting glimpse of Wagner's own hand, or at least the hand which reached its maturity in *Tannhäuser* and *Lohengrin.*

In the same year, 1834, Wagner became chorus master and as-

At a hostelry in Teplitz (far left), Wagner worked on a comic opera, Das Liebesverbot *(The Ban on Love), based on Shakespeare's* Measure for Measure *and musically influenced by Bellini. Insufficient rehearsal turned the premiere at Magdeburg, on March 29, 1836, into a fiasco, with the tenor forgetting his lines and hiding behind a feather boa*

sistant conductor with the Bethmann Company at Magdeburg. This was the start of five years as a conductor in the German provinces during which he acquired a thorough grounding in the general repertoire. He was a born score reader; he could at times risk conducting a work which he scarcely knew. (His very first conducting assignment was *Don Giovanni.*) But he was underpaid, and so continued to borrow money whenever he could: he was inexorably progressing towards the first major crisis of his career, and there began a series of events which was to lead to his exile five years later at the age of twenty-six. Yet his powers of persuasion (and, let us not forget, his conducting abilities) must have been enormous. He had only been at Magdeburg for a few months when he was promoted to chief music director, whereupon he sponsored a concert with very expensive artists and promptly lost a lot of money for the company. In the following year he promoted a benefit concert for himself with his youthful idol Schröder-Devrient as the soloist, and including Beethoven's Battle symphony which, because of its sheer noise, drove the audience away. The concert lost money and his creditors were waiting. He borrowed again from his brother-in-law to finance a tour in search of singers for the company, but this landed him further in debt as the expenses far exceeded his estimate—assuming that he ever made an estimate, which he probably did not.

At the same time he had fallen passionately in love with a young actress in the company called Minna Planer. Her response was at first cool. For one thing she was in great demand by managements; for another, she was in a position to name the parts she wanted to play and the conditions she required. She handled her private and professional life with a composure that was at an opposite pole from Wagner's recklessness. She was almost four years older than Wagner, and had had an illegitimate daughter when she was sixteen whom she always passed off as her sister. Minna was not particularly interested in music, except inasmuch as it led to a living; and she was fully aware of Wagner's perilous financial state—by 1836 he was being threatened with legal action and faced the possibility of imprisonment. Yet, although by no means short of admirers, she could not fail to be impressed by the deluge of passionate letters in which Wagner begged her to marry him. It was a tumultuous relationship from the start.

In March 1836, when Wagner was twenty-three, the premiere of *Das Liebesverbot* took place in Magdeburg. It was a disaster. The singers had not adequately studied their parts, and when a sparse audience gathered for the second performance (which was to be a benefit for Wagner), it was cancelled because of a matrimonial dispute among the artists. Even

In time Wagner was to regard Das Liebesverbot *as a sin of his youth, consigning it to oblivion. Not until 1972 was the opera staged in Bayreuth, at the city auditorium by the twenty-second International Youth Conference. Shown here are Mariana with Isabella (Elaine Watts and Anne Conoley) and Friedrich (Steven Henricson), demanding the death penalty for "free sensuality"*

before that, Minna had had to sell a bracelet to redeem the music from the copyist. The Magdeburg company, already close to collapse, went bankrupt, and Wagner took off hastily for Berlin, leaving his creditors in disarray. By then he was finding it increasingly difficult to borrow from anyone, including his family, and Minna had left to appear in Königsberg. Eventually a friend took pity on him and lent him the money to follow her, and this time she could not refuse him. On November 22 Richard Wagner and Minna Planer were married in the Tragheim Church in Königsberg; the day after the wedding he had to appear before the magistrates and attempt to account for his debts in Magdeburg. His only security was that he had gained the minor post of second conductor at the Königsberg theater, and although in the following year he became first conductor he could find no way to pay off his debts in Germany. There was only one escape route open to him, which was to look abroad in the hope that, communications being what they were in those days, it would take some time for his financial reputation to catch up with him.

He had already written to Scribe, the leading French playwright and librettist, but had received no reply. His next move was to send Scribe a score of *Das Liebesverbot* with a request that it should be submitted to Meyerbeer and Auber for comment. Again there was no reply, and financial pressures were mounting. By April 1837 Minna could stand Wagner's insecurity and outbursts of jealousy no longer, and left for her parents' home in Dresden. There then began a chase which, were it not for the tensions involved, would verge on the edge of farce. Wagner tried to follow Minna, but at once ran out of funds. He returned to Königsberg and sold the wedding presents, on the proceeds of which he went first to Leipzig and then to Dresden, in pursuit of Minna who at first would not budge—and who could blame her? Wagner went to Berlin and met the manager of the theater in Riga, who offered him the music directorship with effect from August. (As Riga was then in Russia and close to the

Pressed by creditors in Riga, where he had been engaged for two years as music director, Wagner fled in 1839 to Paris. There his modern, grandiose ideas and life-style with Minna were lampooned by caricaturist E. B. Kietz (left). Here too, during a two-and-a-half-year residence, he first met Franz Liszt, who was to become a friend, apostle and in-law

Baltic, it provided a convenient geographical barrier between Wagner and his creditors.) He obtained a passport and a contract and went back to Dresden to collect Minna, who at last agreed to go on holiday with him; but they quarreled before long, and Minna left for Hamburg to stay with one of her past lovers.

In August Wagner took up his appointment in Riga. Minna wrote to beg forgiveness, and so he arranged for her and her sister (whom he had already engaged to sing in Riga) to join him in an attempt to make a fresh start. While all this was going on he was reading Bulwer-Lytton's romantic novel *Rienzi,* and considering it as the basis for his next opera; he was also conducting concerts (which sometimes included his own music), and the kind of operatic repertoire demanded by the public—the works of Bellini, Donizetti, Auber, Herold, and Adam—which was not, by itself, to his own taste. His attempt to force the management to promote more serious works was the beginning of his downfall in Riga; that, and the scandal created by his old creditors in Magdeburg and Königsberg, who had at last tracked him down and started legal action. In March 1839 he received notice that his post in Riga would be terminated in June, and his passport was confiscated at the demand of the creditors.

His only hope was to get away, and his object was to get to Paris. He and Minna set about disposing of their assets in secret, including some of Minna's theatrical costumes and the furniture from Königsberg (bought originally on credit, or on borrowed money which had not been returned). Even at this late hour, and despite his reputation for bad debts, he still managed to borrow some more in Riga, and with the help of an old and devoted friend from Königsberg made his escape in a carriage with Minna and a huge Newfoundland dog they had acquired (called, not inappropriately, Robber). The flight across the Russian frontier to an East Prussian port began in September and was made in appalling conditions. They traveled by night, and only on roads and tracks where they were least likely to meet patrolling cossacks. At one stage the carriage overturned

When the Metropolitan Opera first staged Rienzi *in 1885, the mezzo-soprano Marianne Brandt sang Adriano (top left). A revival of the work at La Scala, Milan, in 1964 featured Raina Kabaivanska as Irene with Gianfranco Cecchele, a tenor, as Adriano (top right). The production, designed by Nicola Benois, cast Giuseppe Di Stefano as Rienzi, shown on his throne observing the Act I ballet (bottom)*

and Minna was badly hurt internally. (It is thought that she may have lost her unborn child in this accident.) But, somehow, they crossed the frontier undetected and reached the small port of Pillau where their faithful Königsberg friend—who, at considerable risk to himself had traveled with them—arranged for their passage to London in a small trading ship with a seven-man crew.

The voyage was a nightmare. Because of weather conditions the crossing took three and a half weeks instead of the usual eight days. At one stage they had to seek shelter in a Norwegian fjord, and from the drama of this situation and the rhythmic calls of the sailors when they cast anchor and furled the sails was born the idea of *Der Fliegende Holländer* (*The Flying Dutchman*). Wagner himself has described in great and probably accurate detail the horrors of the crossing; but even in such circumstances the creative process was still at work. *Rienzi* was not finished, but *Holländer* was conceived.

Eventually they reached London and, after a short rest, set off for Boulogne. By one of those amazing strokes of luck which seemed to befall Wagner just as regularly as his misfortunes, he met on board the ferry a Jewish woman who not only knew Meyerbeer, but gave Wagner a letter of introduction to him, adding that Meyerbeer was staying in Boulogne at the time. Wagner and Minna accordingly settled just outside the town while he completed the second act of *Rienzi* in full score. Armed with that and the letter of introduction, he called on Meyerbeer and played through some of the music. Meyerbeer must have been impressed, for he gave Wagner precisely what he wanted—a letter of introduction to the director of the Paris Opera. To Wagner this must have seemed like deliverance indeed. He had escaped his creditors and from the provincialism of the German theaters; he was on the threshold of Paris, armed with a letter of introduction from Germany's most famous composer in France. He had, he thought, arrived; he had no conception of the terrible times that lay ahead.

Celebrity came to Wagner with the premiere of Rienzi *at Dresden's Court Theater, October 20, 1842. The composer had adapted his five-act libretto from a tragic novel by Edward Bulwer Lytton. The original title hero, tenor Joseph Tichatschek, is shown here with Henriette Kriete, a later interpreter of the trouser role of Adriano*

II

THE PIVOT POINT

PARIS at that time was the center of the operatic world, and Wagner at the age of twenty-six and with his tribulations seemingly behind him was ready to conquer. He was quickly disillusioned. He spoke very little French, and the scores he submitted made little impression. There was a glimmer of hope when, as a result of Meyerbeer's introduction, the Theatre de Renaissance accepted *Das Liebesverbot*; but it promptly went bankrupt, and that was the end of that.

Such good fortune as he found came through friends introduced by his sister Cäcilie, who had by then married and whose husband worked in Paris. He borrowed from all of them; he pawned all of his and Minna's possessions, and then sold the pawn tickets. Indeed, the year of

Der Fliegende Holländer *(The Flying Dutchman), adapted from legend, came to Wagner as an idea during his stormy sea voyage from Latvia. Here is the 1975 production by the San Francisco Opera, designed and directed by Jean-Pierre Ponnelle, who makes the action the nightmare of a sleeping sailor, with the Dutchman's coat lined with treasure (inset Theo Adam)*

The theme of the libretto of Der Fliegende Holländer—*salvation of a lost man by a loyal woman—later was to appear in Wagner's* Tannhäuser. *Shown above, the self-sacrificing Senta hurling herself into the sea*

1840 was among the most desperate of his life, for within six months of his arrival in Paris he was again hopelessly in debt to a new set of creditors. He managed to sell the plot of *Der Fliegende Holländer* to the Paris Opera, which was then, to Wagner's humiliation, set to music by Pierre Dietsch. He resorted to any kind of hack work—choruses for vaudeville, songs, selections from popular operas for all sorts of vocal and instrumental combinations—and yet somehow, amazingly, never lost faith in his own work. He completed the first version of his *Faust* overture, and

1ᵗᵉ Vorstellung im vierten Abonnement.

Königlich Sächsisches Hoftheater.

Montag, den 2. Januar 1843.

Zum ersten Male:

Der fliegende Holländer.

Romantische Oper in drei Akten, von Richard Wagner.

Personen:

Daland, norwegischer Seefahrer. —	Herr Risse.
Senta, seine Tochter. —	Mad. Schröder-Devrient.
Erik, ein Jäger. —	Herr Reinhold
Mary, Daland's —	Mad. Wächter.
Der Steuermann Daland's. —	Herr Bielezizky.
Der Holländer. —	Herr Wächter.

Matrosen des Norwegers. Die Mannschaft des fliegenden Holländers. Mädchen.
Scene: Die norwegische Küste.

Textbücher sind an der Kasse das Exemplar für 2½ Neugroschen zu haben.

Krank: Herr Dettmer.

Einlaß-Preise:

	Thlr.	Ngr.
Ein Billet in die Logen des ersten Ranges und das Amphitheater . .	1	—
Fremdenlogen des zweiten Ranges Nr. 1. 14. und 29.	1	—
übrigen Logen des zweiten Ranges . . .		20
Sperrsitze der Mittel- u. Seiten-Gallerie des dritten Ranges . .		12½
Mittel- und Seiten-Logen des dritten Ranges . .		10
Sperrsitze der Gallerie des vierten Ranges . .		8
Mittel-Gallerie des vierten Ranges . . .		7½
Seiten-Gallerie-Logen daselbst . . .		5
Opern-Loge im Cirkel . . .		20
Parterre-Logen . . .		15
Parquet . . .		10

Die Billets sind nur am Tage der Vorstellung gültig, und zurückgebrachte Billets werden nur bis Mittag 12 Uhr an demselben Tage angenommen.

Zum Verkauf der Billets gegen sofortige baare Bezahlung findet in der, in dem untern Theile des Opernhauses befindlichen Expedition, auf der rechten Seite, nach der Elbe zu, früh von 9 Uhr bis Mittags 12 Uhr, und Nachmittags von 3 bis 4 Uhr statt.

Alle zur heutigen Vorstellung bestellte und zugelegte Billets sind Vormittags von 9 Uhr bis längstens 11 Uhr abzuholen, außerdem darüber anderweit verfüget wird

Der freie Einlaß beschränkt sich bei der heutigen Vorstellung bloß auf die zum Hofstaate gehörigen Personen und die Mitglieder des Königl. Hoftheaters.

**Einlaß um 5 Uhr.   Anfang um 6 Uhr.
Ende gegen 9 Uhr.**

*The Dresden Court Opera staged the world premiere on January 2, 1843
(playbill above), with the noted Wilhelmine Schröder-Devrient (above right)
as Senta. Soon after, Wagner was appointed Royal Kapellmeister there*

by September *Rienzi* was finished except for the orchestration. He had a
first, casual meeting with Liszt, neither of them realizing how much their
lives would become intertwined in later years. But in November his debts
in France caught up with him, and he was sent to a debtors' prison where
he proceeded to complete the scoring of *Rienzi*. Minna wrote desperate
letters to all and sundry about his plight, and three weeks later enough
money had been raised to bail him out.

It is time to consider the extraordinary loyalty of Minna in partic-

ular and of his friends in general, for nobody *except Wagner himself* had sound reason to believe that he was anything more than a victim of acute overambitiousness. His ideas were unwanted, and the resources required by his works were unrealistic. Yet he persisted in the face of everyone and everything, and it is impossible not to admire him for that. His capacity for work (work, that is, which was not likely to be immediately productive) was astonishing. His reading at that time led him to the subjects of *Tannhäuser* and *Lohengrin*, while all the time he was writing the text and the music of *Der Fliegende Holländer*, on the orchestral sketch of which he noted "No money again!" But the breakthrough came in the middle

A Wagner disciple, Anton Seidl (above), conducted the first performance of Der Fliegende Holländer *at the Metropolitan Opera in 1889. The company's outstanding interpreter of Senta during the 1930s was the Norwegian soprano Kirsten Flagstad (inset right). Also shown here are Friedrich Schorr as the Dutchman with Ivar Andersen as Daland (right)*

of 1841 when, as a result of Meyerbeer's recommendation, *Rienzi* was accepted for production in Dresden. This was just what he needed to restore the confidence of his family and friends, and he bombarded all of them with letters about the forthcoming production. He also sent off the score of *Der Fliegende Holländer* to Berlin—a more prestigious house than Dresden—along with another letter of recommendation from Meyerbeer, who seems at that time to have been Wagner's staunchest professional supporter, but whose efforts received no thanks from Wagner later on; indeed, he and his music became the targets for some of Wagner's most vicious attacks.

The miserable two and a half years in Paris came to an end in April 1842, when Wagner and Minna set off for Dresden and *Rienzi*, which was to be the first triumph of his career.

The premiere of *Rienzi* lasted about five and a half hours, and for subsequent performances Wagner made several cuts. (An experiment was made to play the work in two parts on successive nights, but it did not appeal to the public.) But *Rienzi*, despite its length, was a huge success and Wagner became the toast of the town. It must all have been especially gratifying for Minna after all the years of humiliation, but the financial problems were far from solved.

Berlin had in the meantime accepted *Holländer*, but kept postponing the production to Wagner's increasing annoyance. He continued to work on the poem of what was eventually to become *Tannhäuser*; and towards the end of the year he withdrew *Holländer* from Berlin and began preparations for its premiere in Dresden in January 1843. It did not enjoy the popular success of *Rienzi*, which is not at all surprising, given the tastes and attitudes of the time and given that, much more than any of his earlier works, it pointed to the Wagner of the future. It was

Tannhäuser *came to the stage of Dresden's Court Opera on October 19, 1845,*
with the role of Elisabeth created by Wagner's niece Johanna (right).
If the music confounded some listeners, this grand romantic opera soon
became Wagner's most popular work. In 1861 at the Paris Opera (inset playbill),
a revised version of the score was staged, with an expanded Venusberg Scene

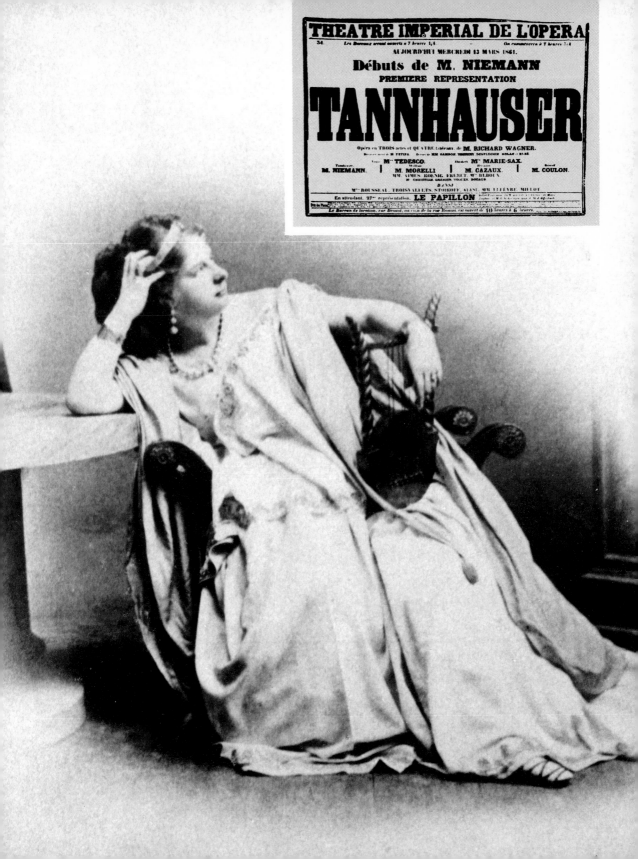

the first of his dramas to be indelibly stamped with the mark of genius, and his first sustained attempt to escape from the French and Italian style of grand opera. Yet it is possible that even he himself did not then perceive the trend in his own work.

He gained a kind of security when, as a result of his brilliant conducting, he was appointed to the post of Royal Kapellmeister which gave him a salary and promised a pension on his retirement. It was far from adequate to provide the lifestyle he required and involved him with far

Two golden ages of Wagnerian artistry have visited the Metropolitan Opera. During the mid-1880s, Albert Niemann (left), Wagner's own choice for the role of Tannhäuser in Paris, sang the part in New York to the Venus of the peerless Lilli Lehmann (below left).
On February 1, 1923, the Czech soprano Maria Jeritza (below center) sang her first Met Elisabeth, to be joined three years later by Lauritz Melchior as Tannhäuser (below right)

The Metropolitan Opera mounted a new production
of Tannhäuser during the 1977-78 season that was
designed by Günther Schneider-Siemssen (sets) and
Patricia Zipprodt (costumes), with direction by
Otto Schenk. Shown here are James McCracken as
Tannhäuser and Grace Bumbry as Venus during
the first act (inset) and the Valley of the Wartburg
in Act III, with Leonie Rysanek as Elisabeth
and Bernd Weikl as the minstrel Wolfram

more conducting than he wished to undertake; but it carried prestige. By the middle of the year he had started the composition of *Tannhäuser*.

His capacity for work remained unabated. When, early in 1844, Berlin at last mounted *Holländer* Wagner conducted the general rehearsal and the first two performances. In March he was in Hamburg to conduct the premiere of *Rienzi* in that city, although neither the singers nor the staging pleased him, and the press was unfavorable. He was called upon to compose a ceremonial piece to mark the return of the King of Saxony from England: it was scored for 120 instrumentalists and 300 singers, and anticipated the rhythm and melody of the Entry of the Guests from Act II of *Tannhäuser*. In September he conducted the twentieth performance of *Rienzi* in Dresden, and by the end of December he had completed all but the scoring of *Tannhäuser*. Such were only some of his activities at the age of thirty-one.

It is, of course, impossible to sustain such a pace indefinitely, and early in summer of the following year his health broke down and his doctor insisted that he needed a "cure" at the fashionable spa of Marienbad. The cure may have rested his body, but it did little to tranquilize his mind. During the period at Marienbad he sketched the poem for *Lohengrin*, for he had taken with him the ancient German epic of that title, as well as Wolfram von Eschenbach's *Parsifal*. (Parsifal was Lohengrin's father.) Thus it can be said that while the poem of *Lohengrin* was being sketched, the idea for what was to be his last work, *Parsifal*, was vaguely taking shape in his mind. And as if all that were not enough, he turned for relief to a comic subject and made his first sketches for *Die Meistersinger*, which was to reach the stage twenty-three years later. He could not be idle.

The premiere of *Tannhäuser* took place in October 1845 with qualified success. The problem lay with the denouement of Act III, for which Wagner composed two further versions during the next two years;

In 1951 at Bayreuth a new look came to Wagner's post-Rienzi operas through the theatrical genius of his grandson Wieland. Using minimal décor, masterly lighting and concentrated acting, Wieland revealed unsuspected depths of meaning even in the early works. Here is his 1964 Tannhäuser, with Leonie Rysanek as Elisabeth, Wolfgang Windgassen as Tannhäuser and Hermann Prey as Wolfram

but that was not the end of the trouble with *Tannhäuser*, as we shall come to see. There were other, exceedingly familiar problems as well. The success of *Rienzi* had been double-edged, for although it had enormously increased his prestige, it had also stirred his creditors into action. In Wagner's view, however, prestige required evidence of a better standard of living, irrespective of past debts. Accordingly, in order to buy suitable furniture and the like, he borrowed from Schröder-Devrient and obtained a considerable loan from the theater pension fund. Worse still, he undertook a disastrous private publishing venture for *Rienzi, Holländer,* and *Tannhäuser,* which he capitalized through further extensive borrowings. The slow acceptance of those works by other theaters put him massively in debt to his new creditors. It has to be said that he displayed as much confidence in such dealings as he did in his creative powers; as he saw it, a loan to Richard Wagner was an investment in the future and therefore, far from being concerned about their money, his creditors should actually be grateful that he had deigned to accept money from them. Everything would be paid off in time (in *his* time); and it would be to their greater glory that they would be able to tell their children, or more realistically their grandchildren, that they had once lent money to Wagner. (A similar attitude, although it has nothing to do with money, explains Wagner's later hostility to Meyerbeer who, during Wagner's unhappy years in Paris, had helped him several times with letters of introduction, recommendations and the like; but Wagner rationalized this kindness by regarding it simply as Meyerbeer's duty when faced with a talent so much superior to his own. Wagner's conclusion that Meyerbeer was a bad composer negated any gratitude for the help that Meyerbeer had given him in lean times.)

In 1846 Wagner was approaching the turning point in his life, and the pivot was *Lohengrin.* He may not clearly have understood what was happening to him, but he followed his instincts. For the first time in his life he composed a major work out of order, and that he did so is significant. It may have had something to do with the troubles he had

Dresden's Court Theater (right), birthplace of three Wagner operas, was not to house Lohengrin's *premiere, which took place in Weimar on August 28, 1850, under Liszt's benevolent baton (inset playbill). When the politically radical Wagner had participated in Dresden's 1849 May Revolution, a warrant was issued for his arrest, and he fled to Switzerland*

experienced with the conclusion of *Tannhäuser*; but whatever the reason, he composed the third act of *Lohengrin* first, then the first act and finally the second. He left the Prelude to Act I until last, which in itself is significant, for it is essentially unlike anything he had written before. It is not a selection of themes from the opera but a kind of tone poem, concerned entirely with the mystical rather than the material aspects of the *Lohengrin* story. It exists to create mood and atmosphere: to suggest that what will eventually be forthcoming will be much more than the necessary but functional setting-up of the story and historical context which occupies much of Act I. In other words, Wagner was developing an aspect of his work that had emerged gradually in the composition of *Holländer* and *Tannhäuser*, and which was to reach its maturity in *The Ring, Tristan,* and *Parsifal.* It was a question of musical and dramatic emphasis, and the relationship between the mystical and the real world. It was an issue that he did not altogether resolve in *Lohengrin*; but *Lohengrin* still represents a gigantic step forward in a new direction.

In January of 1848 his mother, Johanna, to whom he had always been deeply attached, died. In March he completed the full score of *Lohengrin*, which, although immediately accepted for production, was later withdrawn by the Court Opera. Nothing, however, relieved the pressure of his debts; and so, disastrously, he hurled himself into politics. It was, he had decided, the *system* that was wrong, more or less on the principle that since it had failed to provide him with whatever he wanted in life it must, by definition, be faulty. He wrote radical documents proposing a theatrical reorganization in Saxony which brought him into headlong conflict with the court authorities (who were of course his employers). He went further by joining an association whose aims included that of arming the populace in order to force the king to abdicate, although he was then to be reinstated as a constitutional monarch at the

Lillian Nordica was the first American to sing at Bayreuth, as Elsa in Lohengrin *in 1894. The diva's garb was less resplendent there than that she had worn at the Metropolitan Opera a few months earlier (left). The Met's initial* Lohengrin *had been staged during its first season, 1883-84, in Italian, with Italo Campanini as the Swan Knight (inset)*

Among the foremost interpreters of Lohengrin *during the '20s and '30s were Karin Branzell as Ortrud (far left), Kerstin Thorborg as Ortrud (top), Elisabeth Rethberg as Elsa (above), Alexander Kipnis as King Henry (top right) and René Maison as the hero (right). Stars of the Metropolitan Opera's 1976 Everding-Lee-Hall production were Pilar Lorengar as Elsa and René Kollo as her groom (far right)*

hands of the people. Wagner made a journey to Vienna because it was the center of political intrigue and unrest, and because he hoped to find support there. He did not, and returned to Dresden disillusioned.

The revolution in Dresden, when it finally came about in May 1849, was short-lived. The king fled, and Wagner supervised the printing of pamphlets urging the Saxon troops to desert and join the "popular" front. There is no doubt that he was in the thick of things and in some danger, and at one point—when he heard that Prussian troops were likely to invade the city—he took Minna to safety in his sister's home in Chemnitz; but then he returned to Dresden. The city was in chaos, and the revolution had crumbled. Worse still, Wagner was now a wanted man who faced charges of high treason because of his direct association with the revolutionaries. The instincts which, in music, had led him steadily if deviously toward fulfillment clearly had no equivalents in his political character. His most urgent objective was to escape arrest, and with that in mind (and the help of his brother-in-law), he went to Weimar to see Liszt, who not only lent him money but suggested Paris as a place of refuge. Armed wth a borrowed passport, Wagner set off through Bavaria and eventually reached Zurich, Switzerland, where he rested for a while before going on to Paris. To his dismay, and despite Liszt's recommendation, he was scarcely more welcome in that city than he had been ten years earlier; so, after greeting old friends and noting with alarm an outbreak of cholera in the city, he went back to Zurich.

Meanwhile Minna had returned to Dresden to deploy their household effects among friends and to send his scores to Liszt in Weimar. She deeply resented the loss of position, and regarded her husband's political views with contempt. It gives some idea of Wagner's financial state to say that when he began his exile in Zurich he left behind him in Germany debts amounting to thirteen times his annual salary as Kapellmeister; but it was not the prospect of facing his creditors that now kept him out of Germany. It was the much more serious charge of political crimes against the realm.

A new staging of Lohengrin *by designer Günther Schneider-Siemssen and régisseur Herbert von Karajan was seen at the 1976 Salzburg Easter Festival with décor like pages from a medieval book of hours. Here are two scenes from Act I and the Act II wedding procession with Karl Ridderbusch (Heinrich), Anna Tomowa-Sintow (Elsa), Siegmund Nimsgern (Telramund) and René Kollo (Lohengrin)*

Wagner's political activities did not stand in the way of his artistic creativity; indeed, to some extent the two were complementary, for since about 1845 he had been steeping himself in German history and legend. He read, among other things, the Volsunga Saga, the Nibelungenlied, the writings of the Grimm brothers and many other versions of the Nordic tales. He wrote a treatise called *Die Wibelungen* (*The Wibelungs*) about German political history expressed in terms of a saga. This was eventually followed by a scenario called "The Nibelung Myth as Sketch for a Drama," from which, very gradually and over many years, there emerged his conception of the *Ring* cycle.

The connection between these writings and his political leanings is direct. He had not, of course, at that stage worked out or even thought out the implications of the Nibelung saga; it was simply that the quest

As a boy, King Ludwig II of Bavaria came under the spell of Wagner's works. Born the year of Tannhäuser's *premiere, he took the throne in 1864 at the age of eighteen (below), offering the composer his patronage. Though their friendship provoked scandal, nothing could sway the monarch's zeal: he fancied himself the collaborator of genius, and in a real sense he was. At right, Ludwig in royal attire*

for the Nibelung Hoard (which was gold) struck him as a symbol of the struggle for power. A simplified Marxist concept suited his position very well, for Marx propounded that the inheritance of wealth and property (and the power vested there) was a fundamental wrong. Wagner had inherited nothing at all, and yet those court officials who could not see their way to grant his talent whatever conditions he felt it required were themselves untalented aristocrats who had inherited wealth. The theory fitted like a well-tailored suit. It also confirmed the reason for the failure of his publishing venture, because the lack of capital had prevented the propagation of his works and consequently held his artistic ambitions in check. Two factors merged to bring out the political revolutionary in Wagner. One was the imaginative impact of legends he had been studying, for within them he could discern some symbolic patterns related to the German people (which gave him comfort, if only by suggesting that his predicament was part of the eternal condition of mankind); the other was the fact that his financial position was now beyond redemption. Nothing less than the downfall of the capitalist society and the substitution of some kind of social revolution, which might pay particular attention to the needs of Richard Wagner, would suffice to get him out of trouble.

The immediate outcome was his exile in Switzerland with a price on his head. And yet from this strange mixture of frustration, despair, opportunism, and sheer doggedness there came eventually an act of creation and an act of deliverance beyond anything that even Wagner could have imagined. The study of the legends and the experience of the revolution led him, after Minna had joined him in Zurich in 1849, to write his essays on "Art and Revolution" and "The Art Work of the Future." He had started a drama called *Jesus of Nazareth* in which Christ was portrayed as a social revolutionary. He wrote an essay on "Jewry in Music" and a self-justification of his political ideas in "A Communication to My Friends."

In the Bavarian Alps stands Neuschwanstein, enduring testimony to King Ludwig's mania for Wagner's output. Rich tapestries, murals and art works depict scenes from the composer's music dramas in this never-never-land castle. Small wonder that Ludwig, who grew more eccentric with the years, was dubbed "the dream king"

These in turn inspired him to write his enormous treatise on "Opera and Drama" in the following year; but behind all this lay the formulation of *Der Ring des Nibelungen.* The act of creation was to take twenty-five years, and the act of deliverance was not to be forthcoming for another fifteen years, but when it came, and in view of all that had happened, it was not without irony: for Wagner's eventual financial salvation was to come from an exalted aristocrat who, save for his love of art in general and for Wagner in particular, symbolized everything which the revolutionaries had fought against and lost.

49

Wagner met his second wife, Cosima, in Paris, when she was only fifteen (with her father, Franz Liszt). Though she first married Hans von Bülow, a conductor who championed Wagner's music (left), she began a liaison with Wagner in 1864 that produced three children as well as a divorce from the forgiving Bülow and much pain for her aging rival, Minna

III

THE CONCEPT OF THE RING

By January of 1850, at Minna's insistence, Wagner was back in Paris again with further financial help from Liszt. His one hope was to write something of immediate appeal to the Paris public, but his choice of subject was unsuitable and his heart was not in the work. He became infatuated with Jessie Laussot, a cultured and musical young lady some seventeen years his junior whom he had met once before, and who was now married to a wine merchant in Bordeaux. (Minna remained in Zurich, in the belief that her husband was at last working on a truly commercial project in Paris.) Jessie returned Wagner's affections, and prevailed upon her mother (who was a very wealthy Englishwoman) to grant Wagner an endowment so that he could continue his creative work in exile.

Mathilde Wesendonk (left, with her son Guido) provided inspiration to Wagner
between 1852 and 1859 as he labored on his Ring *cycle and* Tristan und Isolde.
Wife of one of his patrons, Otto Wesendonk (inset), she wrote poems for five
songs he composed. She also caused bitter jealousy in Minna, who died in 1866.
By then, Cosima had preempted Wagner from both Mathilde and Minna

Thus began another almost farcical adventure. Jessie naively identified herself with Swanhilde, the bride of Wieland the Smith, the opera on which Wagner was supposed to be working. He knew perfectly well that he would never finish the piece, but convinced himself that he and Jessie should elope to Greece and the Orient (on Jessie's mother's money) to seek a "sublime creative lifestyle." Unfortunately, or perhaps fortu-

Wagner sent this portrait of himself by Friedrich Pecht to King Ludwig, having the artist paint a bust of the regent by his left hand (below). The composer's "music of the future" demanded much of an audience, with its philosophical and compositional complexities and heavenly length. In Paris, Gustav Doré caricatured the public before and after a typical Wagnerian experience (below right)

nately, Jessie confided in her mother who promptly told her son-in-law, Jessie's husband, who had also been the recipient of her financial help. He announced that he would shoot Wagner on sight if he came near Bordeaux, which did not prevent Wagner from going there to explain himself: but the Laussots had left town. Wagner then returned to Paris and, without mentioning Jessie, wrote to Minna to say that he could not continue his life with her. She was immediately suspicious and went to Paris to find her husband who, needless to say, had gone into hiding. There were several further developments in this subplot before Wagner eventually returned to Zurich and made a temporary peace with Minna.

That incident is only worth recounting in this brief survey of Wagner's life because it shows his need for the kind of "inspirational" companionship which the long-suffering Minna could not provide. She could not comprehend the nature of his dilemma; neither, perhaps, could he, but it was none the less genuine. As a dramatist he was moving in an entirely new direction, not with the abandoned *Wieland the Smith* but with the poem of *Siegfried's Death*, which had been inspired by his readings of the legends and sagas, and which was now in its fourth version. The trouble was that it would not take a musical shape in his mind; it would not adapt to any of the existing operatic forms. Even an elaboration or extension of the *Lohengrin* format was useless. Hence, at that time, his need to pour out his feelings in letters and essays, not so much for the benefit of the recipients as in an effort to clarify his own thoughts. In particular, his letters to his closest friend Theodor Uhlig in the Dresden orchestra reveal his state of mind.

The environment was not helpful, either. Zurich at that time was a provincial town with only slight musical activity to which Wagner contributed what he could by conducting the standard repertoire in the small theater. One encounter of major significance for the future came about with the arrival of Hans von Bülow, a pupil of Liszt's, who survived for only a short time in Zurich but whose ability as a musician and conductor impressed Wagner from the start. Meanwhile, in Weimar, Liszt himself was preparing for the premiere of *Lohengrin,* even though the forces at his disposal were woefully inadequate for so difficult and demanding a piece. Wagner, still in political exile, obviously could not attend, but he sent Liszt all sorts of suggestions in the hope of making the premiere a success. It turned out to be more than that: it was a breakthrough, for whatever the disadvantages imposed by the lack of resources at the tiny Weimar theater, Liszt's production proved that Wagner's operas could be played effectively in smaller theaters. From that time onward the demand for them spread throughout the German provinces; but

Tristan und Isolde, *whose chromatic harmonies expanded the horizons of music, was first given June 10, 1865, at the Court and National Theater in Munich, with Ludwig and Malvina Schnorr von Carolsfeld as the tragic lovers (right), Bülow conducting. For a year Wagner and Cosima had lived royally in the city, thanks to the unstinting generosity of their patron, King Ludwig*

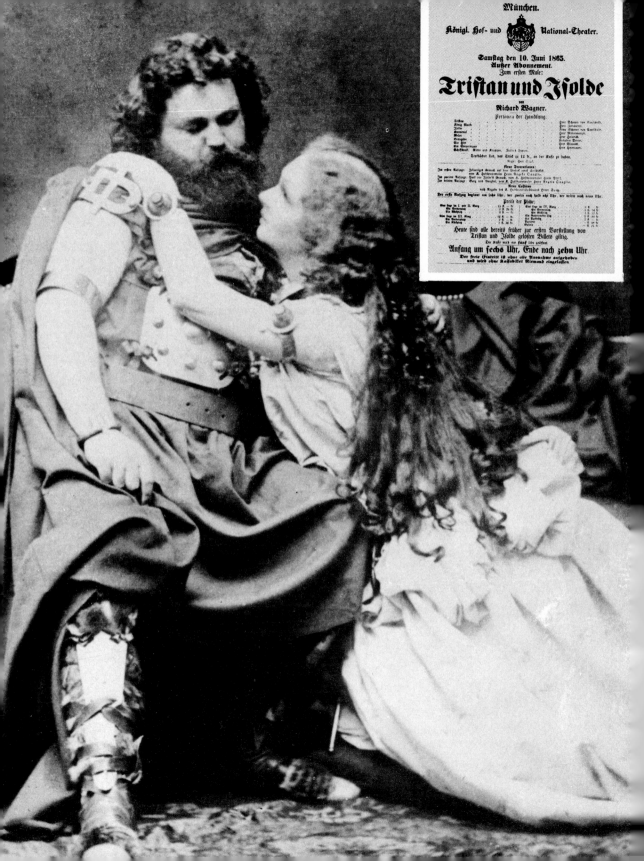

Wagner, pleased though he was by this belated recognition, was as always thinking more of the future than the past.

The vast project taking shape in his mind was *Der Ring des Nibelungen* (*The Ring of the Nibelung*). So different in style, concept, and above all size was this from all his earlier work that it would not come within the scope of any existing theater, and in 1850 he wrote to his Old Paris friend Kietz outlining some first thoughts for the construction of a temporary, wooden festival theater properly equipped to house the work. (Another twenty-six years were to pass before such a building— though not temporary—was to open in Bayreuth with the first complete performance of *The Ring*.)

At first Wagner had thought of one work, to be called *Siegfried's Death,* the poem of which he had finished in first draft form in 1848—six months before his enforced exile. We know how he was then diverted by other matters (the attempt to write for Paris, the affair with Jessie Laussot, the various essays, and above all his book *Opera and Drama*), but in the back of his mind was the thought that too much was left unexplained in *Siegfried's Death,* despite constant revisions. Accordingly, in May 1851 he started work on a prose sketch which he called *Young Siegfried*. It was only when this had been completed that he finally glimpsed the reality of his project, for just as *Siegfried's Death* required the explanations provided by *Young Siegfried,* so the latter would itself require explanation through another work. Thus was born the idea of the Nibelungen saga in the form of three dramas and a prologue, the texts of which he had in effect written backwards. The poems for *Die Walküre* (the first drama) and *Das Rheingold* (the prologue) were completed in the summer and fall of 1852; and in the final months of that year he revised the two Siegfried dramas into something very similar to what we now know as *Siegfried* (originally, *Young Siegfried*) and *Götterdämmerung* (originally *Siegfried's Death*).

The enormity of the project was quite beyond Minna's com-

Kirsten Flagstad and Lauritz Melchior hold the all-time house records at the Metropolitan Opera for the roles of Isolde and Tristan. The soprano sang Isolde there on fifty-five occasions, the tenor appeared as Tristan on ninety-seven. As a team, these matchless artists from Scandinavia sparked a renaissance of interest in Wagner's music dramas at the Met during the late 1930s

prehension, and—it must be admitted—beyond that of most of Wagner's friends. It was not just the scale of the work that they found difficult; it was the mixture of myth and reality, the underlying symbolism which scarcely related to anything in the familiar operatic repertoire. And what theater would ever mount such a project, and which management would find the money? In 1853 Wagner arranged for the original poems to be printed and circulated privately to his friends; and then on four evenings he read them aloud on two different occasions, first to a small group in the Hotel Bauer au Lac in Zurich and then to a larger gathering in the Casino. Among the audience on the first occasion was a lady who was to play a major role in his later emotional and creative life: she was Mathilde Wesendonk whom he had met one year earlier on the occasion of a performance of the *Tannhäuser* overture. Mathilde was then twenty-three and married to Otto Wesendonk, a wealthy silk importer and merchant. They lived in the Bauer au Lac, which fact alone indicates the standard of luxury to which they were accustomed.

Shown here are moments from the historic 1971 Metropolitan Opera production, Tristan und Isolde *designed by Günther Schneider-Siemssen and directed by August Everding :* Mignon Dunn as *Brangäne trying to console Birgit Nilsson as Isolde in Act I (top left); the impassioned love duet— Liebesnacht—of Tristan and Isolde in Act II (bottom far left); and Jess Thomas as the mortally wounded Tristan yearning for Isolde during his third act delirium (above)*

Wagner was approaching his fortieth birthday, and the occasion was marked by three festival concerts in which he conducted excerpts from *Rienzi, Der Fliegende Holländer, Tannhäuser,* and *Lohengrin* (the first time, incidentally, that he had heard any substantial sections from that work). Friends in Dresden tried to gain a political amnesty for him, and were thanked for their efforts by the reissue of the arrest warrant. Otto and Mathilde Wesendonk remained staunch friends and supporters, and Wagner wrote a piano sonata for Mathilde—the first music he had written for five years, since the completion of *Lohengrin.*

His comings and goings, and his trials and troubles over the next few years can only be briefly sketched. What matters is that, despite all that was going on, he started the composition of *The Ring;* and for that he needed to indulge in luxurious living, as his friend Liszt noted after spending eight days with him in Zurich in the summer of 1853. Minna, now in ill-health, worried persistently about money, so Wagner went off mountain climbing with a friend in Italy. (It was after a boat voyage to La Spezia towards the end of the holiday that the E flat music at the start of *Das Rheingold* first came into his head.) He went back to Zurich to start work, but found that Minna had gone on a cure; he therefore went off to Basle where Liszt was giving a concert, and found himself in the company of devoted admirers, including von Bülow, Joachim, and Cornelius. He read them the revised version of *Siegfried,* and then decided to accompany Liszt to Paris where he met, for the first time, Liszt's daughter Cosima. She was sixteen. He also met Liszt's mistress, Princess Wittgenstein, and to both of them he read the rest of *The Ring.* The Wesendonks were also in Paris, and there were many friends from old times to be re-encountered. Minna joined him and, predictably, he spent a great deal more money than he could afford.

He returned to Zurich in November and began the composition sketch of *Das Rheingold.* On the strength of more borrowings from Liszt and Wesendonk he furnished a new house to provide the lavish environment he felt appropriate to his creativity, but by then even their generosity was under some strain. His Dresden creditors began pressing again, and he tried to borrow from his niece Johanna. His fame was now considerable, but his financial situation was, if anything, worse than ever.

By mid-January 1854 he had finished the composition of *Das Rheingold* and the full score was completed by September. In the meantime he began to compose *Die Walküre;* he also read Schopenhauer's "The World as Will and Idea" and this, together with his increasing infatuation with Mathilde Wesendonk, prompted the first ideas for an opera on the subject of Tristan and Isolde. (Schopenhauer, to whom Wagner sent one of the privately printed copies of the *Ring* texts, seems to have been less impressed by the work than horrified by Wagner's solecisms in

Jon Vickers (below left) has laid a claim on the role of Tristan in recent years, singing it with distinction at the Metropolitan Opera, in his native Canada, Europe and South America. On the international scene during the 1950s and '60s, a frequent exponent of Isolde's handmaiden, Brangäne, was the distinguished German-born mezzo-soprano Christa Ludwig (below right)

German.) But (and it is almost unimaginable that it should be so) the idea of *Tristan* was beginning to take shape while Wagner was still less than halfway through *The Ring,* for which there were no production plans whatsoever, except for the vain hope expressed in a letter from Wagner to Liszt that it might be produced in 1856. Where, how, and with whose money was quite another matter.

In 1855, in the hope of earning some money, he accepted a conducting invitation from the Philharmonic Society in London. There were eight concerts spread between March and June and, because he had been unaware of the high cost of living in London, his profits were negligible. The programs were extremely long in accordance with the custom of the time, but he had a success with the public if not with the critics. He met Queen Victoria and Prince Albert; he dined with Berlioz and was introduced to Liszt's pupil Karl Klindworth, who in later years was to prove invaluable in making piano reductions of Wagner's scores.

He returned to Zurich and the business of scoring *Die Walküre.* Meanwhile, Munich produced *Tannhäuser* in August and repeated it nine times; Berlin presented the work the following January. Royalties were beginning to come in, but not sufficiently to grant him the independence he desired. After interminable negotiations, the publishers Breitkopf and Härtel withdrew their offer to publish *The Ring* (although they had heard none of the music) on the grounds that no theater known to them would be likely to mount so extravagant a work. But Wagner went on. He finished the full score of *Die Walküre* in March 1856; he sketched out a drama on a Buddhist subject *Die Sieger* (*The Victors*) which he then set aside; considerations of *Tristan,* encouraged by his emotional involvement with Mathilde Wesendonk, were never far from his mind; and he began work on the composition of *Siegfried.*

Meanwhile Otto Wesendonk had built a large villa in the Enge district of Zurich which had a summer house in the garden, and this he put at the disposal of Wagner and Minna. They moved in before the Wesendonks took possession of the main house, and it was there that

A new production of Tristan und Isolde *was unveiled in 1972 at the Salzburg Easter Festival, with décor by Günther Schneider-Siemssen and staging by Herbert von Karajan. Here are the first-act encounter of the lovers (top, Jon Vickers and Helga Dernesch) and the barren wastes of Kareol in Act III, where in despair Tristan awaits the arrival of Isolde*

Wagner took one of the most momentous and amazing decisions of his life. He decided, at least for the time being, to abandon *The Ring*. In June 1857, when he was rather less than halfway through Act II of *Siegfried,* he wrote to Liszt: "I have led my young Siegfried into the beautiful forest solitude. There I have left him under a linden tree and, with tears from the depths of my heart, said farewell to him." (The truth is that one month later he did complete the second act; but then he put the entire *Ring* aside.) From its inception *The Ring* had occupied him for nine years; it would be another twelve years before he began Act III of *Siegfried.*

All sorts of factors impinged to bring about this situation. His relationship with Minna was worsening; there seemed to be little chance of getting *The Ring* staged, even if he could complete it, because he had reached a sort of musical and dramatic impasse. He needed time for thought and a greater maturity to tackle the ideas—but most of all he needed more than ever to apply himself to the composition of a work within the resources of the average theater. The Wesendonks had by then moved into their villa, and the proximity of Mathilde provided him with the emotional and spiritual impetus he needed. He plunged at once into work on *Tristan und Isolde.* He also set to music five of Mathilde's poems—the Wesendonk Lieder—and two of them are clearly "studies" for *Tristan.* The music of *Tristan* was unlike anything he (or any other composer) had ever written and was to have a profound effect on the music of the future. It was composed with an indescribable passion, and that passion has lost nothing with the passing of the years.

There was one other event that summer which was to have profound reverberations in the future. Hans von Bülow had married Liszt's daughter, Cosima, and during their honeymoon they came to visit Wagner and Minna at the Wesendonks' estate. Nobody present could have had the slightest intimation of what was to happen within seven years.

By the beginning of 1858 Wagner was feeling the need for a change, and for a while he went to Paris. For one thing, he felt that his benefactor, Otto Wesendonk, stood in the way of his "idealized" relationship with Otto's wife, Mathilde. Minna was becoming increasingly suspicious. Yet on the professional front things were looking up. Munich had presented *Lohengrin* to enormous public acclaim, and the work seemed ready for the same kind of recognition that *Tannhäuser* had already received. Furthermore, Breitkopf and Härtel paid him a substantial advance on his new "practical" opera, *Tristan und Isolde,* not realizing, perhaps any more than did Wagner at the time, that the work would be far too difficult, musically speaking, to be seriously practical except for major houses in a position to engage outstanding singers. It is a problem that remains to this day.

Wagner returned to the Wesendonk summer house, and sent a sketch of the prelude to *Tristan* with a long letter to Mathilde, which Minna intercepted and read. It was no more an ordinary love letter than *Tristan* is an "ordinary" love story, but it was quite enough for Minna: she was tired, ill with heart disease, losing her looks, and seemed to be about to lose her husband to a woman half her age. The severance (if that is the right word) between the two families was civilized, amounting to little more than an understanding that Mathilde would not visit Wagner in the summer house. It is impossible not to sympathize with Minna, except that if she had been able to comprehend something of the nature of *Tristan und Isolde* she might have understood a great deal more about her husband's relationship with Mathilde. Otto Wesendonk was prepared to overlook and play down the affair; but that did not satisfy Minna, who returned sadly to Germany.

Wagner, still working on *Tristan,* visited Venice, Zurich, and Geneva. March of 1859 found him in Lucerne where he and a housekeeper occupied an entire floor of the Hotel Schweizerhof. He visited the Wesendonks again and somehow persuaded Otto to advance considerable money against the publishing rights in *Das Rheingold, Die Walküre,* and the unfinished *Siegfried.* Thus fortified he returned to work on *Tristan,* and at the close of the score he wrote "Lucerne, August 6th, 4:30 p.m." And then this most unpredictable of men again did the unpredictable. He did not resume work on *The Ring* or give further thought to the abandoned *Die Sieger.* Instead, he decided on two things: he would try once more to conquer Paris; and try to bring about a reconciliation with Minna.

IV

THE ROYAL BENEFACTOR

THE second objective proved easier than the first. Minna joined him in Paris, but in musical terms the city was still Meyerbeer's stronghold and Wagner, although by now a celebrity in his own right, was not welcome in all circles. He financed and conducted a series of concerts to promote his own music which was a public success, a critical failure, and another financial disaster. He was received by Berlioz, Gounod, Saint-Saëns, and the aged Rossini, and decided after that to try another concert series in Brussels. It too was a financial failure.

He was able to redeem some of these losses by selling the publishing rights of *The Ring* to Schott of Mainz, from which firm he took a considerable advance on *Das Rheingold* with a supplement from a wealthy lady Wagnerite. He conveniently forgot to repay the advance he had al-

Wagner, who suffered from an irritating skin disease, felt most comfortable garbed in silks and furs. His rich dress and other less defensible extravagances did not endear him to the citizens of Bavaria, who through King Ludwig footed the bills. Thus on December 10, 1865, the composer was exiled for political and financial reasons, moving from Munich to a villa in Switzerland

ready received from Otto Wesendonk. When Wesendonk, with a mixture of amazement and bewilderment, challenged Wagner about the repayment of the advance he found himself offered a promissory note for *Siegfried's Death*, the final part of *The Ring*, although Wagner had not by then composed a note of the work. Yet Wagner's attention was soon diverted from such squalid matters by the enthusiasm of Princess Metternich, the wife of the Austrian Ambassador in Paris, for *Tannhäuser,* which she had heard in Dresden. She in turn was a great friend of the Empress Eugenie of France, and thus a production of *Tannhäuser* at the Paris Opera was ordained by the imperial command of Napoleon III.

Wagner proceeded at once to modify his work extensively. After the overture he wrote a brand new Bacchanale, a wild balletic orgy scene with music which relates more to his *Tristan* idiom than to anything in *Tannhäuser* itself; he greatly extended the opening scene between Venus and Tannhäuser; and he made changes in the second and third acts. It was a major operation, but there was a piece of good news at the end of it: Germany had granted him a partial political amnesty which allowed him to travel where he wished except in Saxony. It was an obvious anomaly for Wagner to be so honored by the French Emperor while remaining a refugee from Germany.

The bad news was to come. Despite careful casting, excellent décor, and a fine orchestra (to say nothing of one hundred and fifty-six piano rehearsals and eight full dress rehearsals), *Tannhäuser* was a fiasco. For once it was not Wagner's fault. The wholly incompetent conductor was Pierre Dietsch who, twenty years earlier during Wagner's first visit to Paris, had set to music the draft text of *Le Vaisseau Fantome* (*Der Fliegende Holländer*) which Wagner had sold to the Paris Opera for a pittance. Yet it was not all Dietsch's fault; a political hostile group had encouraged powerful elements in French high society (and especially in the Jockey Club, which subscribed heavily to the opera) to rally against *Tannhäuser* in general, and in particular against Wagner's in-

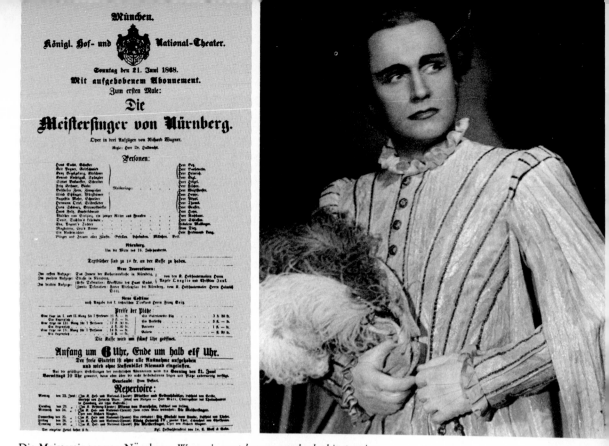

Die Meistersinger von Nürnberg, *Wagner's great human comedy, had its premiere in Munich on June 21, 1868, with the composer in the royal box as guest of King Ludwig. He had portrayed himself onstage in the character of Walther, a young minstrel who breaks new paths in music. Shown above is a famous Metropolitan Opera Walther of the 1940s and '50s, the Swedish tenor Set Svanholm*

sistence that he would not provide a ballet scene where custom had always demanded it: in the second act, so that the nobility could dine out during the first. The performances were disrupted, and Wagner withdrew his work after the third. It was the biggest scandal in the history of the Paris Opera, and *Tannhäuser* was not revived there for thirty-four years.

To some extent his disappointment was mitigated during a trip to Vienna, when he heard *Lohengrin* for the first time (thirteen years after its completion!). *Holländer* also had a triumph in that city. Yet the fiasco of *Tannhäuser* in Paris had taught him a lesson, which was that compromise had no part in either his character or his work. He wrote to

Mathilde Wesendonk that, after such an experience, he had only to glance at *Tristan* and the incomplete *Ring* to ask himself: "Where have you been? You have been dreaming! Open your eyes—*this* is reality!"

But there was another kind of reality to be faced. Liszt and other friends again helped him with money, but he now knew that Minna's heart condition would no longer allow her to spend even part of her life with him. He wanted her to return permanently to Dresden, where he would make her a modest settlement for the rest of her life. What he did not know, and what he could not have imagined, was that in the city of Munich his eventual benefactor was hearing *Lohengrin* for the first time. He was fifteen and a half.

Wagner's creative impulse never lay dormant for long. A visit to Nürnberg reminded him of the sketch he had made sixteen years earlier for a comedy to be called *Die Meistersinger*. He returned to Paris and completed the poem in thirty days; then, in January 1862, he moved to Biebrich near Mainz to begin composition of the music. Minna, unannounced, joined him there, but their relationship was now too fragile to survive for more than a mere ten days: the arrival of a parcel from Mathilde Wesendonk was enough to spark off old jealousies, and Minna took herself off to Dresden again.

In March Wagner recived his full amnesty from the Saxon king, which meant that he could travel anywhere in the land of his birth, but his money problems were as acute as ever. He lived a restless, itinerant life—borrowing, scrounging, and demanding as best he could. He had affairs with a young girl from Mainz and an actress from Frankfurt, but in November he went to Dresden for what was to be his last meeting with Minna. From there he went to Vienna in the hope that rehearsals for *Tristan* were progressing seriously, which they were not, and so for the next year he lived as an itinerant conductor, touring in Germany, Austria, and Russia. On his way to Russia he visited Hans and Cosima von Bülow in Berlin, and he stayed with them again in November. These encounters portended more than anything else that year, for they marked the beginning of the most profound relationship of his life: he had fallen in love with Cosima, and she with him. On November 28 he wrote: ". . . with tears and sobs we today sealed our confession to belong to each other. . . ."

Wagner's home at that time was in Penzing, outside Vienna, but early in 1864 the pressure from his creditors was such that the only option open to him was flight. (Vienna had abandoned the production of *Tristan*.) He was literally at the end of his resources, and his reputation was such that he could no longer borrow; he was in love with another man's wife; and the music of *Die Meistersinger* remained unfinished. He fled to Germany and then to Switzerland and then back to Germany. His letters during this period are those of a man driven to the edge of despair, and yet there is always a note of defiance, of arrogance, rather than self-pity. It was the spark that kept him alive—the total self-certainty that his kind of genius could not be allowed to perish, and that somehow, somewhere, deliverance would be at hand.

At the end of March 1864, when Wagner was on the run, Crown Prince Ludwig became King of Bavaria on the death of his father, Maximilian. Although he was only eighteen and a half he had been passionately interested in Wagner for more than five years. He had heard *Lohengrin* and *Tannhäuser*, and immersed himself in Wagner's prose writings; he read the public issue of the *Ring poems*, and took particular note of Wagner's call for a special German festival theater "under the patronage of a noble German Prince." Within five weeks of coming to power Ludwig determined to realize Wagner's dreams, and dispatched his cabinet secretary to search for the composer.

He eventually tracked down Wagner in Stuttgart, where at first

the composer tried to avoid him because he might be an emissary from the army of creditors. Then the miraculous truth emerged: Wagner was summoned to Munich by the new king, who wished to relieve him of all financial worries and to create for him the environment and the lifestyle through which he could continue his work. As a token gesture, the cabinet secretary there and then presented Wagner with a portrait photograph of Ludwig and a precious ruby ring. Thus in one stroke was Wagner's life changed, for whatever problems lay ahead he would never again lack financial security, nor would he be at the mercy of creditors. It is fascina-

The Metropolitan Opera first mounted Die Meistersinger *during its third season, 1885-86, with Auguste Seidl-Kraus as Eva and Emil Fischer as Hans Sachs (left). The renowned Czech tenor Leo Slezak sang his initial Walther at the Met in 1910 (below left), while an irresistible Eva at the theater during the 1930s was Lotte Lehmann (below right), whose teacher, Mathilde Mallinger, was Wagner's first Eva*

ting (but pointless) to speculate on what might have happened to Wagner had Ludwig not ascended to the throne at the moment when Wagner's fortunes were at their lowest. It was indeed deliverance. It was veritably too good to be true.

Wagner had his first audience with the king on May 4, 1864. He was offered everything he needed to pursue a creative life. The Villa Pellet near the king's residence on the lake of Starnberg was provided for his sole use; he was given a generous allowance and enough money to go to Vienna and pay off all his debts. In return, the king did not ask Wagner to perform any specific duties: all he required was that the manuscripts of all future works should be his property, and that Wagner should discuss with him in detail his future ambitions so that the king might find a way to bring them to fruition. Ludwig and Wagner were to be partners in what they felt to be the most ambitious artistic project ever conceived.

Yet although Wagner's circumstances had radically changed, his character had not. To treat Ludwig with courtesy and to confide in him artistically was the very least that might be expected of him; but it was inevitable that, sooner or later, Wagner would take advantage of Ludwig's generosity. Despite his regular meetings with the king, he felt lonely at the Villa Pellet: he needed female company, and in June Cosima von Bülow arrived with her two children, aged one and four. Hans von Bülow arrived a week later, but there was no attempt to disguise from him the affair between Wagner and Cosima; it was in fact during this period that she conceived Wagner's child, who would later be named Isolde. The attitude of Hans von Bülow presents another extraordinary aspect of the situation, for he both loved his wife Cosima and positively venerated Wagner. The conflict of emotional attachments led him, not surprisingly, to a nervous breakdown.

Ludwig bought a house for Wagner in Munich which, with seemingly unlimited funds at his disposal, Wagner proceeded to decorate in his most lavish style: he surrounded himself with the best silks, satins, and

When Wagner created the role of the pedantic town clerk
Sixtus Beckmesser in Die Meistersinger, *he in fact parodied one*
of his harshest critics, Viennese writer Eduard Hanslick (inset).
At the turn of the century at the Metropolitan Opera, the most popular
singer of Beckmesser was the American bass David Bispham (left)

velvets from his Viennese milliner. Hans von Bülow was appointed court pianist by Ludwig, which served a double purpose: it would help to improve the king's musical education, but it would also bring the von Bülows to live in Munich, where Cosima could spend more time with Wagner and help him to choose the decorations for his new home. At that period Wagner's work consisted of scoring Acts I and II of *Siegfried*, and discussing with Ludwig the plans to build a festival theater in Munich for the performance of his forthcoming works; it was to have an invisible orchestra. Other plans included the foundation of a new music school to prepare for Wagner's conception of the German art form of the future.

With Hans Sachs, Wagner created one of the major roles in the bass-baritone repertory. Shown below, Friedrich Schorr, the Metropolitan Opera's sage cobbler in thirty-five performances of Die Meistersinger *starting in 1924*

But Wagner's growing influence with Ludwig had not escaped the notice of the press. He had made enemies in the court, and those enemies were all too ready to leak information, true or untrue, which might reflect badly on the king's favorite. It was not just that Wagner seemed to have unlimited access to Ludwig's money: beyond that, it was felt (and with some justice) that he was wielding political influence over the young king. He was incapable of suppressing his arrogance. He boasted that he could twist the director of the Hoftheater round his little finger, and he made the foolish mistake of referring to Ludwig as "mein Junge" ("my boy") in the presence of the same cabinet secretary who

The American singer Thomas Stewart added the character of Sachs to his many Wagnerian credits at the Metropolitan Opera in 1976 (below). The role was based by Wagner on a historical shoemaker who wrote over 6,000 poems

At the 1975 Easter Festival in Salzburg, *a new staging of* Die Meistersinger *came to the boards, the work of designer Günther Schneider-Siemssen, with Herbert von Karajan as director. Shown at left is Act II, a townscape of old Nuremberg with Karl Ridderbusch as Hans Sachs seated outside his shoeshop musing on Walther's trial song. Musing on other trials, no doubt, is Wagner himself in this photograph by Joseph Albert (below), taken in Munich in 1865. The composer's dog Pohl rests at his master's feet, and other notable faces in the group include those of Hans von Bülow, directly behind Wagner, and Leopold Damrosch, third from the right*

had brought him from Stuttgart for his first meeting with the king. Needless to say, the remark was passed on to Ludwig and led to the first of many temporary disruptions in his relationship with Wagner. It is hard to imagine why a man of Wagner's intelligence behaved over and over again with such crass stupidity. Because of Ludwig's devotion and protection he doubtless felt invulnerable; but he reckoned without the power of the press and of those at court, who saw his extravagance and influence as a menace to the state.

In April 1865 his daughter by Cosima was born, and von Bülow accepted her as *his* own third daughter. In June, von Bülow conducted the premiere of *Tristan and Isolde* which, because nothing like it had been heard before, left the public bewildered and the press more hostile than ever. The tragic death of the tenor Ludwig Schnorr von Carolsfeld, who created the part of Tristan, less than three weeks after the last performance stunned Wagner and von Bülow. They set off for Dresden to attend his funeral, but arrived too late. Although news had reached Wagner that Minna was dying, he did not bother to visit her when he was in Dresden. Perhaps he feared that she might make unacceptable demands, for he had tried to conceal the extent of his vastly improved circumstances. In a letter to a friend she wrote: "Every three months I get a crumb from Richard's abundance."

In the first flush of his new affluence Wagner had paid off most of his Viennese creditors, but by the middle of 1865 there were others determined to receive their due, some of them stretching back as far as his Dresden and Paris days. He therefore demanded more money, and this time the king hesitated, though not for long. Ludwig did not himself discuss such menial matters: he merely gave approval and delegated the affair to court officials. Wagner sent Cosima to collect the money which he expected in the form of banknotes, but the treasury officials took what revenge they could by paying out the huge sum in sackfuls of silver coinage. Cosima had to hire two carriages to transport the money.

The Schneider-Siemssen and Karajan staging of Die Meistersinger, *1975 Salzburg Easter Festival : Act I in the church, with Walther (René Kollo) testing for the Masters; the Act III quintet in Sachs' shop, with the cobbler (Karl Ridderbusch), Magdalene (Kerstin Meyer), David (Peter Schreirer), Eva (Gundula Janowitz) and Walther; and the meadow outside Nürnberg during Act III, Walther's Prize Song*

„Habt Dank der Güte
aus tiefstem Gemüthe!
Und darf ich denn hoffen
steht heut' mir noch offen
zu werben um den Preis,
daß ich Meistersänger heiß?"
„Oho! Fein sacht!" etc. etc.
(Siehe Textbuch der Meistersinger 2ᵗᵉ Ausgabe Seite 23.)

King and composer maintained their regular meetings, when they discussed philosophy, poetry, and the art forms of the future. Wagner went to stay with Ludwig at his castle in Hohenschwangau and arranged for wind players to waken them with the "Morgengruss" fanfare from *Lohengrin*. After Wagner had left, Ludwig dressed his young adjutant as Lohengrin and had him drawn by swans in a model boat across the Alpsee. It is perhaps no wonder that court officials were concerned for the priorities, if not also for the sanity, of their monarch. But the persistent attacks in the press began to wear Wagner down, if only because, although spiteful, they were true. He then made his biggest blunder by publishing an anonymous article in a Munich paper in which it was claimed that Wagner and Ludwig could only pursue their artistic aims if two or three court officials who opposed those aims were removed from their positions. The implication was that their dismissal would be in the best interests of the Bavarian people.

Nobody had the slightest doubt about the author of the article or of the identity of the officials; and this time Wagner had gone too far. The officials, backed by the royal family and the archbishop, petitioned the king for the removal of Wagner—and at last Ludwig grasped the danger of his own position. He sent his second cabinet secretary (the first was one of those whom Wagner wanted dismissed) to tell Wagner to leave Bavaria for six months, and before dawn on December 10 Cosima and his friends saw him off to Switzerland. But this was a different kind of exile from all the others, because Luwig had provided him with money to go where he liked and to live in the style he expected. He had plenty of work to complete, including an autobiography which he had started to dictate to Cosima in the summer. Six weeks after he left for Switzerland, Minna died in Dresden.

At the premiere of Die Meistersinger, *Wagner stepped forward in the royal box to accept the homage of the public. A caricature with verse soon appeared, parodying the moment : "Thank you for your goodness, out of the depths of my heart! And may I hope that I have a chance today to compete for the prize to be called a Mastersinger. Oh! What a nice thing! etc. etc."*

V

BAYREUTH

IT was a relief for Wagner to get away from the Munich intrigues. He took a villa on Lake Geneva and resumed his work on *Meistersinger*, but the villa was too cold for him; he moved over the border into France and settled for a time in Marseilles. Contact with Ludwig was maintained by regular correspondence, though he and Wagner often resorted to code names in case, as they suspected, their letters were being intercepted. Cosima and her three daughters joined Wagner in March, and soon afterwards they found a house on a peninsula opposite Lucerne. It was called "Triebschen," and it was there that Wagner was to spend one of the happiest and most productive periods of his life. Ludwig sent him the annual rent as a gift, and once again Wagner set about the business of ordering his favorite satins and silks.

The Margraves' Opera House, a baroque theater designed by Bibiena, seemed a logical site for the Bayreuth Festival, which Wagner conceived in 1870. Ultimately, he felt its décor too ornate for high-minded German art and proposed building a new theater. Shown here are interior and exterior views of Bayreuth's "other" theater, a marvel of Italianate architecture

The separation was harder for Ludwig than for Wagner, and in May the king elected to make a secret visit to Triebschen to be with Wagner on his birthday. It was an ill-judged move: inevitably and predictably the news leaked out in Munich, and at the very time that hostilities were about to be declared between the Austrians and the Prussians. Bavaria had thrown in its lot with the Austrians, and within a few months was to suffer a humiliating defeat at the hands of the Prussians, who demanded and received heavy reparations and some territory. Before that— indeed at the time of his visit to Wagner in Switzerland—Ludwig was already contemplating abdication. He had little interest in the main issues of kingship, and wanted to devote even more of his life and money to the realization of Wagner's plans; but Wagner was astute enough to see that he needed Ludwig rather more as a king than as a friend.

At this time, when relations between the Bavarians and Prussians were worsening daily, Hans von Bülow (who was a Prussian) found himself under constant attack in the Munich press. It was claimed that he and Cosima were deceiving the king in order to remain in his favor, while relieving Ludwig of a great deal of money to help Cosima's "friend," who was, of course, Wagner. To stifle this scandal Wagner, through Cosima, persuaded Ludwig to send Bülow a letter (with permission to publish) denying all the charges, and confirming that Bülow and Cosima were a noble and devoted couple, whose friendship with and loyalty to Wagner was only to be understood in terms of art. The letter ended with the king's assurance that those who had spread the malicious gossip about Wagner and Cosima (who had already borne him one child and was now pregnant with another), would be brought to justice. The letter was published, but its impact was lost because it appeared three days after war broke out with Prussia. Had that not been the case, an astute journalist might have discovered the truth—which was that Wagner himself had dictated the letter, which was subsequently signed by Ludwig.

In 1866 Wagner had settled in a peaceful villa at Triebschen, near Lucerne (right). Here King Ludwig secretly visited him. Here too Cosima gave birth to Eva (inset with papa) and Siegfried, and for Cosima's thirty-third birthday Wagner wrote the Siegfried Idyll, *drawing on motifs from the nearly finished* Siegfried, *third part of his cycle* Der Ring des Nibelungen

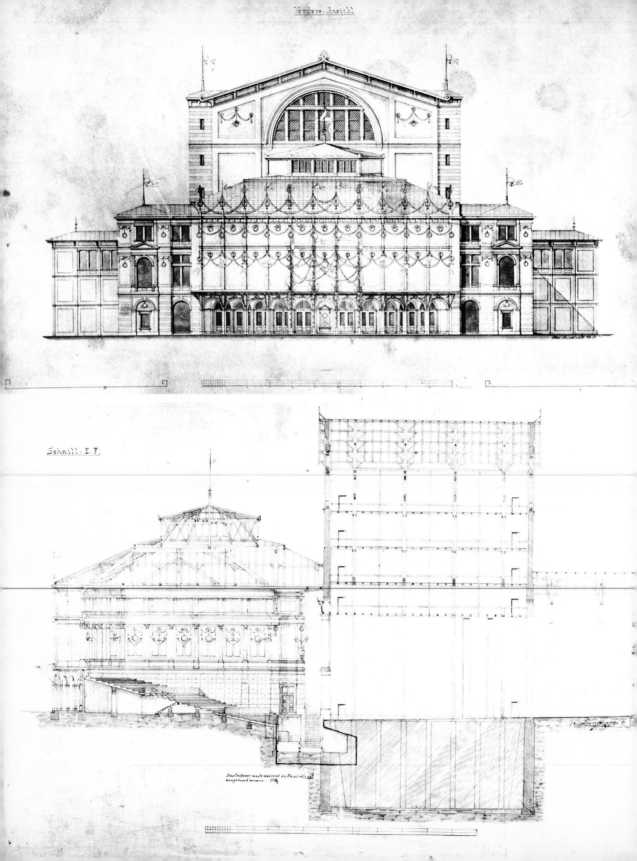

Vordere-Ansicht

Schnitt- E. F.

Das Orchester musste während des Baues alle mal
vergrössert werden.

This act of disloyalty through which Wagner and von Bülow and Cosima compromised their benefactor indicates the extreme to which they were prepared to go to protect their own reputations.

When the brief war was over, von Bülow joined Cosima and Wagner in Triebschen to work out the next moves. It was essential to maintain von Bülow's official position in Munich in order to ensure the proper presentation of Wagner's works in that city and to proceed with

89

"Away with the ornaments!" wrote Wagner on a design by architect Otto Brückwald for the front façade of the Bayreuth Festspielhaus (top left). The theater, built to the composer's specifications, was adapted from one planned for Munich, with the orchestra hidden from sight (bottom left). In 1872 Wagner led Beethoven's Ninth Symphony at the Margraves' to mark the laying of the cornerstone (below)

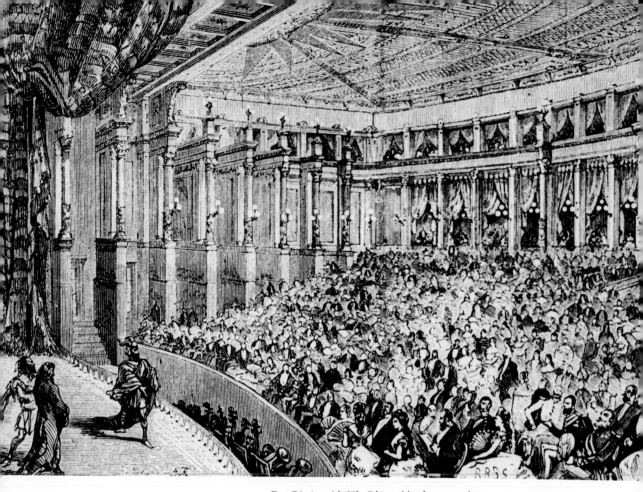

Das Rheingold (The Rhinegold), first part of Wagner's magnum opus, a four-evening setting of the ancient Nibelung Saga, inaugurated the fan-shaped, acoustically ideal Festspielhaus on August 13, 1876 (above)

the foundation of the new music school; and now that Minna was dead and buried, it was time to arrange for Wagner to marry Cosima. An unusual degree of ingenuity would be required in order to avoid another scandal. To add to the problems, Ludwig was having another bout of abdication fever, but Wagner again dissuaded him: he offered the suggestion that Ludwig might make Nürnberg the center of political and cultural power in place of Munich, and that the royal residence might be located in the small town of Bayreuth.

Wagner continued to work on *Meistersinger*, and in February of

Between the audience and the stage at Bayreuth's festival theater is a
"mystic abyss," where orchestra and conductor work unseen. Shown above,
Wagner looks in on a rehearsal through a window in the hidden pit

1867 he completed the composition sketch for Act III; in the same month his second daughter, Eva, was born at Triebschen. A month later Wagner visited Munich for an audience with Ludwig to discuss the forthcoming production of *Meistersinger*; later he stayed with the king at Schloss Berg and for his birthday Ludwig gave Wagner a unique combination desk and piano to provide greater comfort during the process of composition. But one thing was becoming very clear: although Ludwig had lost none of his passion for Wagner's works and ideals, he was no longer prepared to be advised on political or governmental matters. It not only

Bühnenfestspielhaus
in Bayreuth.

Aufführungen am 13.–17., 20.–24. u. 27.–30. August

Richard Wagner's Tetralogie
Der Ring des Nibelungen.

Erster Abend: Rheingold.   Dritter Abend: Siegfried.
Personen.   Personen.

Zweiter Abend: Walküre.
Personen.

Eintritts-Karten (½ Patronatschein) zu beziehen durch den
Kölner Richard Wagner-Verein.

had to be, but had to be *seen* to be, that he was not under Wagner's influence in those areas.

Lohengrin was produced at the Munich theater in June, and *Tannhäuser* in August, both under the direction of von Bülow. At Triebschen, Wagner finished *Meistersinger* in October. At that point another plan was born, which was to start a newspaper in Bavaria in which Wagner, although resident in Switzerland, could air his views on art and politics. His chosen editor was subsidized by royal patronage, and when Ludwig received advance copies of the last two of twelve articles Wagner had written he promptly pronounced a veto on their publication. (They contained criticisms of church and state and a particularly vicious attack on the French which might have caused a diplomatic crisis since the paper was subsidized indirectly by the government.) Once again, Wagner showed that he could not keep himself out of the political arena for long.

For a while relations with Ludwig were strained, but by May 1868 the friendship was established again and Wagner spent his birthday with the king. A month later *Meistersinger* received a triumphant premiere in Munich, tarnished only by the fact that Wagner sat alongside Ludwig in the Royal Box and shared the ovation with the king. This was considered an appalling breach of etiquette and provided plenty of fodder for the press; but nothing could stop the success of *Meistersinger* which, during the next two years, was produced all over Germany and in Vienna. Wagner reacted violently to the personal attacks in the press, and vowed never again to attend performances of his works in Munich.

Gossip about Wagner's relationship with Cosima was now flowing freely. Liszt, Cosima's father, had known about it for some time, and it was a double embarrassment to him since he had taken on minor Catholic orders. Although Cosima was still living in Munich with von Bülow, news of the affair inevitably reached Ludwig's ears, and was confirmed

A tricky scenic effect in Das Rheingold *is the illusion of mermaids swimming beneath the Rhine. At the Bayreuth premiere, Minna Lammert with Lilli and Marie Lehmann (top right) rode on ribbed bunks elevated on poles attached to hand-maneuvered dollies (bottom). Lilli Lehmann survived the adventure to sing Brünnhilde at the 1896 Festival*

Das Rheingold, *Scene 1, under the Rhine in contemporary stagings—at Salzburg by Günther Schneider-Siemssen and Herbert von Karajan, with water nymphs circling gold as Alberich glowers in the depths (top); London's Royal Opera by director Götz Friedrich, with eel-like maidens of designers Josef Svoboda and Ingrid Rosell; New York's Metropolitan Opera by Schneider-Siemssen and Karajan, with Zoltán Kelemen as Alberich on the verge of stealing his all-powerful prize (right)*

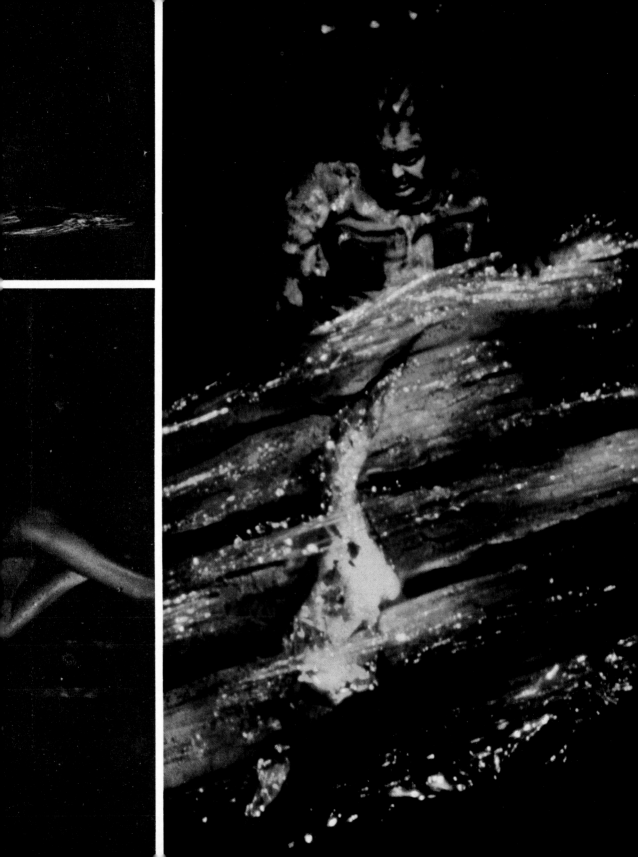

when Wagner wrote to him and suggested that Cosima should leave Munich forthwith. The king did not agree. The issue was complicated because under Prussian law, von Bülow could not obtain divorce on the simple grounds of desertion; on the other hand, an admission of adultery by Wagner and Cosima would not only unleash an avalanche of publicity but would inevitably compromise the king, if only because of the "white wash" letter which he appeared to have written to von Bülow two years earlier.

The Metropolitan Opera's 1912 lineup of gods waits to pass into Valhalla, with William Hinshaw as Donner, Carl Burrian as Loge, Hermann Weil as Wotan, Margarete Matzenauer as Fricka, Alma Gluck as Freia and Lambert Murphy as Froh (below). When World War I began, Wagner's works were banned from the Met, and no gods crossed over the Rainbow Bridge until the season of 1924-25

The continuing scandal forced Cosima to leave Munich. She joined Wagner at Triebschen, after which they went on holiday to Italy. When she returned to von Bülow in Munich she did not tell him that she was pregnant by Wagner for the third time. Her final break with von Bülow came in December 1868. Meanwhile, Wagner's relationship with the king had deteriorated, and there was some concern on Wagner's side that his allowances might be withdrawn; but, after a gap of twelve years, he returned to the composition of *The Ring*. He added some finishing

The world premiere of Das Rheingold *took place not at the first Bayreuth Festival but seven years earlier in Munich, on September 22, 1869 (below). From 1899 to 1932 at the Metropolitan Opera, the ranking earth goddess Erda was the eloquent German contralto Ernestine Schumann-Heink (below right), who was seventy when she made her Met farewell as this character in* Siegfried

touches to Act II of *Siegfried* and then started immediately on the composition of Act III.

Wagner and Cosima's third child, Siegfried, was born at Triebschen on June 6, 1869. Hans von Bülow resigned from his Munich position on hearing the news, but Liszt sadly accepted the inevitable and agreed that his daughter should renounce her Catholicism and marry Wagner as soon as possible. Ludwig was more concerned with preparations for the premiere of *Das Rheingold* in Munich, with which he was determined to go ahead despite von Bülow's resignation and Wagner's outright opposition, and so there began a classic battle of wits between Wagner and his patron. Wagner's talented pawn in this game was the musician Hans Richter, who had worked for some time as a copyist at Triebschen, and who went to Munich to take over the *Rheingold* production. As Wagner's representative his brief was simple: if anything at all failed to match Wagner's expectations, he was to sabotage the production. In due course he informed Wagner that although the musical standard was satisfactory the stagecraft was not, which was scarcely surprising since he had refused to cooperate with the theater management from the start. Richter recommended a concert performance and, when his suggestion was rejected, promptly resigned. Wagner, still in Triebschen, seemed to have won.

Ludwig, however, had had enough. To Wagner's fury he merely postponed the premiere to give time for the stage machinery to be put in order, and handed over the conductorship to Franz Wüllner, the chief repetiteur in Munich. Wagner went to the city in an attempt to intercede, but Ludwig refused to see him. The breach with the king was now serious; he wrote no letters to Wagner for four months. But Ludwig was adamant and *Das Rheingold* received its premiere on September 22; it was a qualified success. Wagner then hit on a simple expedient to prevent a complete performance of *The Ring* in Munich: he would withhold the full scores of *Siegfried* and *Götterdämmerung* until Ludwig's thirst to

98

Das Rheingold was rethought at the Metropolitan Opera in 1968 as part of a modern staging of the Ring *cycle. In the final tableau, the gods— Wotan (Thomas Stewart), Fricka (Josephine Veasey), Froh (Donald Grobe) and Freia (Simone Mangelsdorff)—ascend to their new home in the clouds, Valhalla. The fire god, Loge (Gerhard Stolze), chooses to remain below*

hear them led him to provide the theatrical conditions that Wagner required. But he could not prevent Ludwig from staging *Die Walküre* which took place, again under Wüllner, on June 26, 1870. In July Cosima secured her divorce from von Bülow, and on August 25, Ludwig's birthday, she and Wagner were married in the Protestant Church in Lucerne. The king cabled his congratulations. For Cosima's thirty-third birthday Wagner composed the *Siegfried Idyll* (originally called the *Triebschen Idyll*) which was played by a small group of musicians on the stairs of the house. (Hans Richter, who was by training a horn player, undertook the trumpet part.)

A regular visitor to Triebschen at that period was the young philosopher Friedrich Nietzsche, whose boundless admiration for Wagner and his works made him an ideal propagandist. The story of the gradual decline in the relationship between the philosopher and the composer would require a book in itself, though the fault was largely on Wagner's side. He was willing enough to accept Nietzsche as a disciple but disinclined to take Nietzsche's own ambitions very seriously. Over a period of some seven years Nietzsche's attitude to Wagner changed from adulation to virulent hatred. In any case it is unlikely that two such volatile temperaments would have sustained a stable friendship for very long, but if Wagner had shown a little more perception or even consideration it is unlikely that Nietzsche would have turned into such an articulate enemy.

Wagner's determination that the first complete *Ring* should not be presented in Munich led him to look elsewhere. He had read about the Margrave Opera House at Bayreuth in northern Bavaria: it was said to have the largest stage (at least in terms of depth) in the whole of Germany, and Bayreuth itself was within Ludwig's domain. Wagner went there on his way to address the Berlin Royal Academy, only to discover that the exquisite theater was unsuitable for his purposes: the rococo au-

The Théâtre National du L'Opéra in Paris undertook a fresh restaging of the Ring *cycle in 1976, a concept that emphasized the greedy bourgeois nature of Wagner's gods. Shown here in* Das Rheingold, *directed by Peter Stein and designed by Karl-Ernst Hermann and Moidele Bickel, are Christa Ludwig as Fricka and Theo Adam as Wotan, garbed in gaudy evening attire*

Die Walküre (The Valkyrie), first staged in Munich on June 26, 1870 (far right playbill), was Bayreuth's second night, with Josephine Scheffsky of the Munich Opera as Sieglinde (above left). On November 25, 1903, this role served for the Metropolitan Opera debut of the Swedish singing actress Olive Fremstad (above right), who was also acclaimed for her moving portrayals of the three Brünnhildes

ditorium was far too small and the stage inadequately equipped and not adaptable. The town of Bayreuth however, appealed to him. It was not so remote as to be inaccessible, and yet it was far enough away from the scandals and intrigues of Munich. He began to devise a scheme to replace Ludwig's idea for a festival theater in Munich, for if such a theater could be built in Bayreuth, which was at the center of the new German Empire,

Over the years Die Walküre *has become the best-loved* Ring *drama, not only for its many pages of excitement and grandeur—the ride of the Valkyries, the magic fire music—but for its ability to touch the heart. Real human need and suffering are expressed in the role of Sieglinde, eloquently sung during the 1930s by the celebrated German-born soprano Lotte Lehmann (above)*

it would attract precisely the kind of audience that Wagner wanted. Only the devoted and the dedicated would make the journey, and their attention would not be diverted by other attractions.

Wagner gained the support of the mayor of Bayreuth and of a local banker. They worked out a plan to enlist one thousand wealthy patrons (later the target was increased to thirteen hundred) who, in re-

turn for their subscriptions, would be guaranteed free admission to the
first festival to be held in the summer of 1873 in the newly built theater.
Wagner wrote enthusiastically to Ludwig, and enclosed a copy of the
orchestral sketch for Act II of *Götterdämmerung* to whet the king's ap-
petite. By that time Ludwig had given up the fight to stage *The Ring* in
Munich, and was becoming the obsessive guardian of his own privacy.
He also realized that Wagner would never honor his Munich contract, and
so capitulated to the Bayreuth idea. He responded by taking out about
eighty subscriptions.

The concept of the Bayreuth festival was daring in more ways than
one. It was not meant to be a "public" occasion at all, but would depend
for its success on the continuing support of its subscribers. The design of
the theater itself would eliminate the compromises imposed on Wagner's
works in ordinary theaters. The fan-shaped, steeply raked auditorium would
provide perfect sight lines from virtually every seat; the backstage area
would be immense and the stage machinery would be the latest and best;
and the orchestra pit would be below audience level and partly covered
by a huge curved cowl. This meant that the orchestra and conductor would
be invisible to the audience, yet able to play at full strength without
drowning the singers. Nothing was to interfere with the imaginary
world of the stage. The nature of the materials to be used in the construction of the building (mostly brick, wood, and plaster) seemed to guarantee
a fine acoustic. Altogether it was a brave and brilliant idea, and history
has vindicated Wagner's faith; yet at the time there were appalling difficulties, which Wagner had to contend with while trying to complete
Götterdämmerung.

In April 1872 he and Cosima said goodbye to their beloved Triebschen and moved into the Hotel Fantasie in Bayreuth. He bought a plot
of land for the house he proposed to build for his family, and on May 22
—Wagner's fifty-ninth birthday—the foundation stone of the theater was
laid. Over the next year he went on frequent concert tours to raise money
for the festival and to try to form Wagner "societies" in the major German

*Patrons of the 1876 Bayreuth Festival heard singers of the highest quality
in the major roles of the* Ring *cycle. Amalia Materna (top right) was the
Brünnhilde, with Albert Niemann (bottom right) as Siegmund, parts that both
artists were later to perform at the Metropolitan Opera. Cast as the father
of the gods, Wotan, was Franz Betz (far right), the first Hans Sachs*

cities. It was from these societies that he hoped to build the subscription audience for the Bayreuth festival, but his ideas did not produce an enthusiastic response: by April of 1873 only two hundred of the proposed thirteen hundred subscriptions had been sold, and it became clear that there would be no festival in that or even the following year.

In May the building of Wagner's new home in Bayreuth began with funds provided by Ludwig, but the situation at the theater looked bad. By June there were just over four hundred subscribers, which was less than a third of the total required. In September Wagner appealed urgently to Ludwig for a further loan in order to continue the building of the theater, but Ludwig refused: by that time he was not only becoming a recluse but was committed to his own castle-building projects at Neuschwanstein and Linderhof (which, with his future "Versailles" at Herrenchiemsee, were to bring him to financial disaster). An approach to the emperor through the Grand Duke of Baden also failed. The building of the theater had been started on promissory notes, and the building fund was by that time deeply in debt to the contractors. Even supposing that money could somehow be raised to finish the theater, further funds would be required to cover interior fittings, stage equipment, scenery, and costumes.

Once again Ludwig came to the rescue with a loan that was large enough to solve the immediate problems, but this time there were stringent conditions. Repayments were to be made within eighteen months; performances were to begin in the following year (1875); all future receipts from the subscribers were to be paid to the treasury, and all fittings in the theater were to be the property of the king until the loan was repaid. It was also made clear that this was to be Ludwig's final contribution. But it seemed that the Bayreuth project had been saved, and in April the Wagner family moved into their new house called Wahnfried.

In October of that year Wagner had to tell Ludwig that the theater would not be finished on time. He added that while it might be possible

Wotan and his favorite daughter : the towering German bass-baritone
Hans Hotter as the errant god, surrounded by four of this century's most
admired interpreters of Brünnhilde—Frida Leider of the 1920s (top left),
Kirsten Flagstad of the 1930s (top right), Helen Traubel of the 1940s
(bottom left) and Astrid Varnay of the 1950s (bottom right)

*The Metropolitan Opera's most recent staging
of* Die Walküre—*Act I, when Jon Vickers as
Siegmund urges Gwyneth Jones as Sieglinde to
flee with him (inset above); Act III, when
Berit Lindholm as Brünnhilde protects Birgit
Nilsson as Sieglinde (inset far right); and
Act III, when amid the flames Thomas Stewart
as Wotan bids farewell to his sleeping daughter,
with Nilsson as the recumbent Brünnhilde*

to hold preliminary rehearsals in 1875, the scenery, lights, and machinery would not be ready until 1876. This information was accompanied by another passionate plea for more money, or at the very least for permission to retain the subscriptions instead of using them to pay off the loan; but no more capital was forthcoming, and Wagner was not allowed to retain the subscriptions.

Meanwhile he completed the scoring of *Götterdämmerung* and on November 21, 1874 *The Ring* was finished. From its inception to its final form it had taken over a quarter of a century, and it remains—despite the controversy it still arouses—the greatest single conception in the history of dramatic music. It is a miracle that Wagner was able to finish the work in such conditions, for although he certainly found peace in his new home, the financial problems of the theater and the projected festival bore heavily on him.

The title role of Siegfried *was taken in stride during the 1920s and 30s by Lauritz Melchior (below left), who sang the hero forty-seven times with the Metropolitan Opera. At the 1896 Bayreuth Festival, Hans Breuer as Mime forged the magic sword (below right). In Bayreuth's 1976 Chéreau-Peduzzi-Schmidt production seen at right, René Kollo as Siegfried confronts Fafner, the dragon*

By February 1875 the number of subscribers was still below half the target figure, and so Wagner once again undertook an exhausting concert schedule to raise funds to pay off the loan. The endless traveling, to say nothing of all the dinners and receptions and fund-raising speeches, drained his energy and left him in poor health. In every city he visited he took time to listen to singers, and in July his chosen soloists assembled at Wahnfried for the first rehearsals. In that month the first acoustic tests were held in the new theater (Alberich and the Rhinemaidens in Scene 1 of *Das Rheingold*), and in August an orchestra of one hundred and fifteen assembled for the first rehearsals. The musicians comprised some of the finest players from all over Germany, and they came to Bayreuth without fees, although their travel and living expenses were paid. From the first note it was evident that the Bayreuth acoustic was unique: it produced a rich, resonant sound quite unlike that of any other opera house in the world.

When the rehearsals were over Wagner took Cosima on holiday to

Designer Günther Schneider-Siemssen's 1972 Siegfried *at the Metropolitan Opera :*
the Act I forest (top left), Jess Thomas as the hero in Act II (bottom far left)
and Birgit Nilsson as Brünnhilde, Act III (bottom right). In 1975 at La Scala, Milan,
designer Pier Luigi Pizzi and director Luca Ronconi had Norman Bailey as the Wanderer
encounter Birgit Finnilä as Erda in a portrait gallery of the gods during Act III (below)

Teplitz (where, sixty-two years earlier, Wagner's mother had made her rendezvous with Ludwig Geyer). He then went to Vienna and heard hugely successful productions of *Lohengrin* and the Paris version of *Tannhäuser*. He was invited back to Vienna to conduct a performance of *Lohengrin* for a benefit in aid of the chorus, and he did so in March 1876. Meanwhile he had been able to send Ludwig the first three volumes of his autobiography, and he earned five thousand dollars from the United States through a commission to write a "Centennial March." He went from Vienna to Berlin to supervise the first performance of *Tristan* in

With Götterdämmerung *(Twilight of the Gods), first heard in Bayreuth on August 17, 1876, Wagner closed his fifteen-hour* Ring *epic, soon the rage of the intellectual world. During the 1890s at the Metropolitan Opera, the brothers Jean and Edouard De Reszke often sang Siegfried and Hagen (below). Now, at the English National Opera, Rita Hunter performs Brünnhilde (right)*

In 1974 the Metropolitan Opera staged a new production of Götterdämmerung, *designed by Günther Schneider-Siemssen. Shown here are Act I, the Gibichung Hall with Thomas Stewart as Günther, Bengt Rundgren as Hagen and Nell Rankin as Gutrune (above), and Act II, Hagen calling the vassals (top right) and then goading Birgit Nilsson as Brünnhilde to take revenge on Siegfried (right)*

that city, from which he earned fees which were badly needed for the forthcoming Bayreuth festival. They were not, however, enough. By the end of May it became clear that there would be insufficient funds to pay the singers, and once again it seemed likely that the festival would have to be postponed. Ludwig responded to a further appeal, and agreed to suspend repayments of the loan until at least eight hundred subscriptions had been sold.

At the beginning of August Ludwig arrived by train to attend the general rehearsals. He had aged considerably, and such was his obsession with privacy that he had arranged to meet Wagner at a small halt outside Bayreuth in the early hours of the morning: he could not face the prospect of any kind of public reception at Bayreuth station. He and Wagner had not met since the premiere of *Meistersinger* eight years earlier. The next day the king took a back route to the theater to attend a private, closed performance of *Das Rheingold* (he had developed a taste for hearing opera in solitude, for he could not bear the distraction of public attention), but he agreed to hear the rest of *The Ring* with the public in attendance because the empty theater was overresonant. These were officially general rehearsals for which tickets were complimentary, but the passes sold on the black market at high prices. Ludwig was so moved by *The Ring* that he determined to come back for the third and final cycle, by which time all the dignitaries he so wished to avoid would have departed.

The premiere itself was attended by the emperor and members of the nobility from all over Europe. It was a double triumph for Wagner, for his massive work made a profound effect, and did so largely because of the energy he had brought to bear on every aspect of the production. He had worked himself to the limit in coaching singers, attending to scenic details and the proper working of the stage machinery while guiding his conductor, Hans Richter, through the complexities of the score. Predictably certain things went wrong, but given the nature of the venture and its financial instability the degree of success was considerable. At the end of the third cycle, for which Ludwig returned as promised, Wagner appeared on stage and received a tumultuous ovation. In his speech, he referred to Ludwig as the "co-creator" of the work.

Thus did the doors of the Bayreuth festival theater open for the first time in 1876; and for the first time the music of *The Ring* was heard in continuity and in its entirety. There was much to be proud of, yet at the end of it all the festival turned out to be a financial failure.

In 1976, to mark the Ring's *centenary as well as its own, the Bayreuth Festival mounted a controversial new staging of the cycle by director Patrice Chéreau and designers Richard Peduzzi and Jacques Schmidt. Here are the Oath on the Spear in Act II, with Karl Ridderbusch as Hagen, Gwyneth Jones as Brünnhilde and Jess Thomas as Siegfried (top), and Brünnhilde's Act III Immolation Scene (bottom)*

VI

DEATH IN VENICE

THE strains of the festival had exhausted Wagner, but he was optimistic about the future. The bulk of the capital expenditure on the theater was now over, and so he reckoned that a further three cycles of *The Ring* in 1877 would help to reduce outstanding debts. With that in mind he went to Italy with Cosima and the children; and he worked intermittently on the poem of *Parsifal*.

His optimism was unfounded, for when he returned to Bayreuth in December the deficit on the festival proved to be so great that it might be forced into liquidation. It would be necessary to turn over to the king the stage equipment that was legally his, and then auction the remainder to discharge the other debts. Wahnfried might have to be sold, and a proportion of Wagner's income set aside for the creditors; it was even

In 1879 Cosima posed for this oil portrait by Franz von Lenbach. That same year, because of poor health, Wagner traveled with his wife to Italy. At Ravello, in an exotic Moorish palace, he found inspiration for Klingsor's magic garden in Parsifal, *while the grand cathedral of Siena became the stage picture for the Temple of the Grail*

suggested that Cosima might hand over the legacy from her mother, the Countess d'Agoult. The only immediate practical step that Wagner could take to delay such dramatic actions was to resume the life of an itinerant conductor, for he was now in a position to command the highest fees whenever he appeared. He made a return visit to London under very different conditions from before; but in his efforts to reduce the Bayreuth deficit in the face of the apathy of his fellow countrymen he was working himself to the point of exhaustion.

He returned to Bayreuth and began the composition of *Parsifal*. All sorts of ingenious attempts to arrange a festival for the summer of

Wagner balances the Festspielhaus (above); the road leading from Bayreuth to theater (right); and the hatted composer at his home, Wahnfried, August 1881. At the rear are Blandine von Bülow, Heinrich von Stein, Cosima and Parsifal's seated designer, Paul Zhukovski. In front are offspring Isolde, Daniela, Eva and Siegfried with pampered pets

1877 came to nothing, for Wagner was trapped: without money to pay off the debts there could be no more performances, but if there were no more performances there would be no revenue. Productions in Munich brought no royalties to Wagner, as the works performed there were Ludwig's property in perpetuity, but there was a growing demand, especially for *Die Walküre*, elsewhere. Hitherto Wagner had insisted that *The Ring* should be performed complete or not at all; now, faced with such financial pressure, he relented and agreed that the works could be played separately. In order to keep the name of Bayreuth before the public even though the doors of the theater were closed he founded a journal called "Bayreuther

*Perspectives of the Festspielhaus in Bayreuth,
where performances start in the late afternoon,
with intermissions running and hour and a half so
the audience can stroll about the landscaped
grounds, enjoy food and drink, purchase souvenirs
and ponder the music drama being offered.
The three views shown here are rear (top left),
side (bottom left) and front (above), where
over the entrance portico musicians step forth
before each act to sound themes from the day's
opera as a signal for the public to take its seats*

Blätter," and there were ambitious plans for the future if money could be raised from some source: *Holländer, Tannhäuser* and *Lohengrin* were envisaged for production in 1880, followed by *Tristan* and *Meistersinger* in 1881, *The Ring* again in 1882 and *Parsifal* in 1883. These were dreams, although in fact Wagner's royalties were steadily increasing and helping, slowly but steadily, to reduce the Bayreuth deficit.

Cosima appealed to Ludwig for help, but there was no hope of any further capital payment. Deliverance this time came through the hands of the intendant of the Munich Opera, Baron von Perfall, who suggested that a ten percent royalty should be paid by the Munich theater on all future Wagner performances until such time as the debt had been cleared. Ludwig accepted the idea, and so once again Wagner and Bayreuth were saved from the brink of bankruptcy. Wagner immediately devoted his attention to the composition of *Parsifal* and the promotion of his new journal; he also had a brief, idyllic affair with a young girl called Judith Gautier who had attended the festival in 1876 and who had sent Wagner a regular supply of perfumes from Paris. Cosima recorded in her diary how much she dreaded the affair; but, unlike Minna in the past, she did not display her feelings.

Wagner's health was gradually declining, and work on the composition sketches for *Parsifal* went slowly. He sent some commemorative lines to Ludwig on May 3, 1879, which was the fifteenth anniversary of their first meeting, but by July it was clear that *Parsifal* would not be finished in time for the proposed festival in 1880. Ludwig agreed to a postponement, for he knew that creativity could not be subject to a timetable. Wagner did begin the scoring of *Parsifal* in August, but his mind was restless: it was during this period that he wrote his famous open letter to the explorer Ernst von Weber against the killing of animals, and especially against Kosher methods of slaughter. The cold weather and the closed theater in Bayreuth—he now called it "the madman's whim"—

Parsifal, *a "consecrational festival play," was first given in Bayreuth, July 26, 1882. Wagner, though often anti-Semitic in his views, invited Hermann Levi to conduct this Christian tale. Shown at right during the baptism scene of the original Good Friday Spell are Amalia Materna as Kundry, Emil Scaria as Gurnemanz and Hermann Winkelmann as Parsifal (right)*

Bühnenfestspielhaus Bayreuth.

Am 26. und 28. Juli
für die Mitglieder des Patronal-Vereins,
am 30. Juli, 1. 4. 6. 8. 11. 13. 15. 18. 20. 22. 25. 27. 29. Aug. 1882
öffentliche Aufführungen des

PARSIFAL.
Ein Bühnenweihfestspiel von RICHARD WAGNER.

Flowermaidens from the 1882 Bayreuth Parsifal *(above left) and Milka Ternina as Kundry (above center, as seductress and hag) in the Metropolitan Opera's first performance, December 24, 1903. The Met premiere stirred controversy because Wagner had wanted his work staged only in Bayreuth. Since Germany had no copyright agreement with the U.S., his heirs were powerless to prevent the New York production*

depressed him, and so in late December he set off once again for Italy. He and the family eventually settled in a villa at Posillipo, which they rented for more than they could afford for six months; Ludwig again came to the rescue with a handsome rent allowance.

Wagner met old friends and made some new ones in Posillipo, and among the latter was Paul Zhukovsky who was a painter and a friend of the novelist Henry James. He was to become the set designer for *Parsifal,*

During the 1930s and '40s at the Metropolitan Opera, the Austrian bass Emanuel List performed the role of Gurnemanz on twenty-three occasions (above right). After Parsifal's *premiere at the theater, because of its religious nature, the work became a favored piece of repertory, returning year after year at Eastertime, with special matinees scheduled for Good Friday*

and he and Wagner found their inspiration for Klingsor's Magic Garden (*Parsifal*, Act II) in the luxurious vegetation of the Casa Rufolo in Ravello, which lies in the mountains behind Amalfi. Yet the Italian climate did not seem to benefit Wagner's health as much as he had expected, and in August, having sent Ludwig the fourth and final volume of his autobiography and having received another generous increase in his allowance in return, Wagner took his family to Siena, where the interior of the cathedral inspired Zhukovsky to make sketches which influenced his designs for the Grail scenes in *Parsifal*.

Wagner's literary efforts from this period did much to damage his reputation in later years. He was not at all inhibited about displaying his private obsessions, and seemingly oblivious to the contradictions between their stringency and the infinitely bendable rules he applied to his own life. "Religion and Art" suggested that the "will to live" can only fulfill itself

No production has so fully captured the mystical eroticism of Parsifal *as the one staged in 1951 at the first postwar Bayreuth Festival by Wagner's grandson Wieland. Here are Gustav Neidlinger as the magician Klingsor, summoning Martha Mödl as Kundry (below left); George London as the Holy Grail's tormented guardian, Amfortas (below right); and Dietrich Fischer-Dieskau as Amfortas with the Grail Knights (right)*

In 1970 the Metropolitan Opera mounted a new production of Parsifal that was designed by Robert O'Hearn and staged by Nathaniel Merrill. Shown here are Klingsor's magic garden from Act II and the Good Friday Spell from Act III (inset), with Helge Brilioth as Parsifal, Christa Ludwig as Kundry and Cesare Siepi as Gurnemanz

Wagner sat for this family portrait in 1873, grouped with the faithful Cosima and his only male heir, Siegfried. A year later the composer began construction of a home in Bayreuth, Wahnfried (Peace from Madness), with magnanimous underwriting from King Ludwig, a bust of whom guards the entrance (right). Allied bombs during World War II caused great damage to the building, which is now a Wagner museum

through a "will to redeem," and culminated in a plea for a return to Christianity through music. Its sequel, "Know Thyself," identified the Jewish race as a potential cause of mankind's downfall, for in Wagner's eyes the Jews represented the evil arising from the possession of gold and property, and the issue of credit through money lending. Coming from one who had spent his entire life on borrowed money, and who had never shown scruples about its source so long as it found its way into his pocket,

◀ *In 1970 the Metropolitan Opera mounted a new production of* Parsifal *that was designed by Robert O'Hearn and staged by Nathaniel Merrill. Shown here are Klingsor's magic garden from Act II and the Good Friday Spell from Act III (inset), with Helge Brilioth as Parsifal, Christa Ludwig as Kundry and Cesare Siepi as Gurnemanz*

the thesis was both offensive and hypocritical. A further essay on vegetarianism predicted the downfall of the Aryan race through the influence of "flesh-eating Jews." It is all but impossible to associate the man who wrote these essays with the man who wrote *The Ring, Tristan, Meistersinger,* and *Parsifal*: indeed, if *Parsifal* had not been still forthcoming it would have been easy to dismiss the essays as the ravings of a mind in disarray.

He was determined that performances of *Parsifal* on stage should be restricted to Bayreuth, and obtained Ludwig's agreement to the pro-

Death came to Wagner on February 13, 1883 —heart failure in Venice.
The next day Augusto Benvenuti sketched him at rest (below left) in
Palazzo Vendramin-Calergi on the Grand Canal (below center).
Five days later in Bayreuth, a cortège bore his remains from the railroad
station (below far right) to rest in a tomb behind Wahnfried

posal, except Ludwig himself was to be able to have private performances in Munich using the Bayreuth apparatus. (The exclusivity of *Parsifal* at Bayreuth was maintained until December 1903 when a "pirated" performance took place at the Metropolitan Opera in New York. That event was made possible by the publication of the miniature score, and from then onward *Parsifal* gradually took its place in the repertoire of the great opera houses.)

In November 1880 Wagner returned to Munich for what was to

be his last meeting with the king. There were public performances of *Holländer* and *Tristan*, and a private one of *Lohengrin*. He then went back to Bayreuth to resume work on *Parsifal* and to select singers for the first performance; he was obliged by virtue of his contract with Ludwig to use the orchestra of the Munich Court theater under its chief conductor, Hermann Levi. Levi's musicianship was never in doubt, but he was a Jew and the son of a rabbi. Wagner's insensitivity even led him to suggest that Levi should undergo baptism before being allowed to conduct *Parsifal*.

Wagner had received a tempting offer to conduct in America which he had to refuse on the grounds of ill health and the pressing need to finish *Parsifal*. In April and May of 1881 he went to Berlin to attend rehearsals and a final cycle of *The Ring*, and on the latter occasion—and in the midst of a huge ovation—he suffered what seems to have been a minor heart attack and was forced to leave the stage. He must have sensed that time was running out. Between July and October he orchestrated Act II of *Parsifal*, and at the end of that task he wrote to Ludwig to say that his health was getting steadily worse. He worked on the rehearsal and performance schedules for the following summer, and then set off with Cosima and the children for Palermo in Sicily, where he worked on the scoring of Act III. From there they journeyed back slowly to Bayreuth, visiting old haunts and old friends. For his birthday in May 1882 Ludwig sent Wagner a pair of black swans and urged him, now that *Parsifal* was finished, to take up the abandoned *Die Sieger*. Wagner replied that *Parsifal* would be his last dramatic work. "Nothing more," he wrote, "is to be expected of me."

The premiere of *Parsifal* on July 26 was a triumph despite the controversy aroused by the portrayal of religious ceremonies on the stage. For once Ludwig was not present: he pleaded ill health, but his withdrawal from the public scene was by then almost complete, and he could no longer face a repeat of the ovations at the first festival—the more so

Wagner's family and friends united to preserve the art and traditions of the Master at Bayreuth. Shown above, the twenty-year-old Siegfried, already a composer-conductor-director-impresario in the making, poses in 1889 with the Ring's first conductor, Hans Richter, Eva, Isolde, Daniela and Blandine. Below, Siegfried at sixty-one in 1930 with another Bayreuth maestro, Arturo Toscanini

Cosima, holding Siegfried's eldest son, Wieland (above left), survived Wagner by nearly half a century, autocratically ruling the Bayreuth domain to the end. She died on April 1, 1930, four months before Siegfried, whose English-born widow, Winifred (above right), took command of the festival until the early 1940s, enthusiastically welcoming the patronage of Adolf Hitler and the Third Reich

since it had been decided, much against Wagner's wishes, to open all but two of the sixteen performances to the general public. The old "subscriber" system was abandoned forever: henceforward the doors of Bayreuth would be open to the world.

During Act III of the sixteenth and final performance of the season Wagner, unseen by the audience, made his way into the sunken orchestra pit and took over the baton from Levi. He conducted from memory from the transformation scene to the end of the opera; it is possible that he knew, or at least sensed, that it would be the last time he would ever conduct one of his stage works. The *Parsifal* of 1882 had been both an artistic and a financial success and so, despite his ailing health, Wagner began to think of future festivals which would present all his works from *Holländer* onward over the next ten years, after which the running of the festival would pass into the hands of his son Siegfried.

In September the family moved to Venice to live in the sumptuous Ca' Vendramin Calergi, a palace overlooking the Grand Canal. Wagner

Heirs of Valhalla : among the joys of being a grandchild of Richard Wagner and growing up around the Bayreuth Festspielhaus was the unparalleled opportunity to dress up as one of the characters from the music dramas. Here, in a fanciful scene from Der Ring des Nibelungen, *are Siegfried and Winifred's offspring—Wolfgang, Verena, Wieland and Friedelind, circa 1925*

wrote more essays and some letters to Ludwig. For Cosima's birthday he prepared to give a performance of his youthful symphony of 1832, but suffered another heart spasm during the rehearsals. Yet he managed to conduct a performance for an intimate circle of friends, including Liszt, at the Venetian opera house La Fenice.

Early on the afternoon of February 13, 1883 came the final spasm. A blood vessel in his heart was ruptured, and he died in Cosima's arms. The world of music was shattered by the news. Ludwig gave orders for the transfer of the body from Venice to Bayreuth under royal protection, and when the train arrived at Bayreuth the station was filled with flowers. A regimental band played Beethoven's funeral march from the *Eroica*

During the postwar era, Friedelind Wagner (above left) ran master classes in conjunction with the Bayreuth Festival, while Wieland (above right) and Wolfgang (right, rehearsing Gwyneth Jones in Die Meistersinger) *took over artistic control from their mother, de-Nazifying and revitalizing their grandfather's music dramas through modern techniques and concepts. Wieland died in 1966*

symphony and the funeral march from *Götterdämmerung*: and then the
open hearse, drawn by four horses, was taken to Wahnfried. Only two
wreaths, both of them from the king, lay upon the coffin.

Richard Wagner was buried beneath a massive stone slab at the
end of the garden at Wahnfried. Forty-seven years later, in 1930, the
ashes of Cosima were buried beside his remains. As for Ludwig, there
was no such longevity. At the time of Wagner's funeral he said: "The
artist whom the world now mourns, I was the first to discover. I rescued
him for the world." And that was indisputably true. In 1884 Ludwig
heard *Parsifal* for the first time at a private performance in Munich; in
1886 he was purported to be insane and removed from power. A few

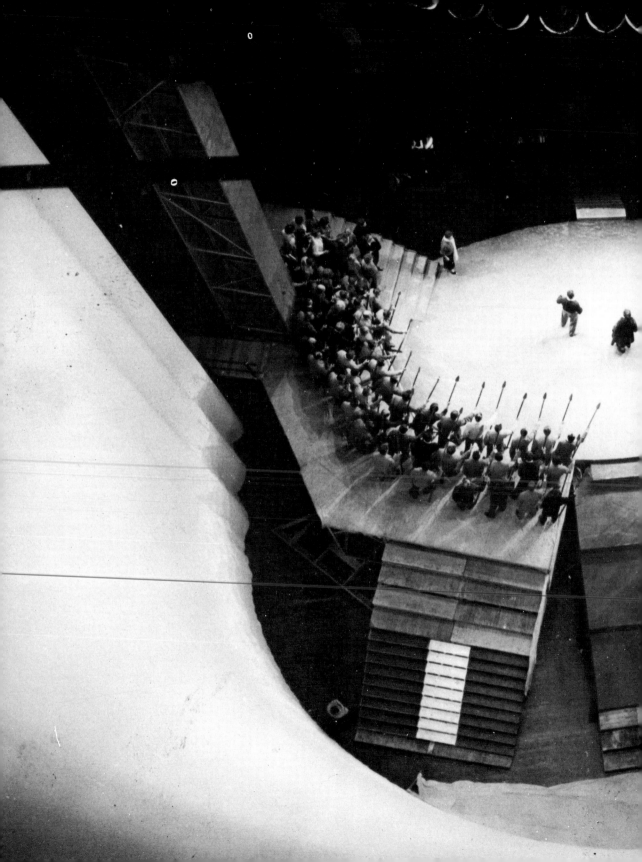

Bird's-eye view of the enormous stage of the Festspielhaus in Bayreuth, encased in the folds of a giant cyclorama, with stairs leading from a lower level to the main playing area, where a rehearsal for Act II of Götterdämmerung *is in progress*

days later his drowned body was found in the Starnberg Lake, although he was known to have been a strong swimmer and was in the company of his doctor, who was also found drowned.

The violent emotions aroused by Wagner and his music during his lifetime exist no less powerfully today, and it is not just the continuation of the family strain that makes his presence still so uncannily evident at Bayreuth. Despite his deviousness, his disloyalty, his ruthlessness and plain dishonesty, he was able throughout his life to command a selfless devotion and love from people who were far from being lackeys. There were those from the early days who lent him money in the knowledge that there was little chance of ever seeing it again; there were those who gave him unstinted hospitality, or who helped him to avoid the authorities when he was in flight. There was Minna, a gifted woman in her own right, who ruined her life, professionally and personally, for him; there were the Wesendonks, who supported him with affection and money; there was von Bülow who lost his wife to Wagner and yet remained devoted to him; there were the musicians—Liszt, Cornelius, Humperdinck, and Klindworth among them—who in varying degrees jeopardized their own careers to serve him; there was Cosima, whose love was such that it could tolerate his most extreme indulgences; and there was Ludwig, the reluctant king who, although finally disillusioned by the endless trickeries of his friend, never for an instant lost faith in Wagner's musical and dramatic visions.

Why did they, and countless others, suffer for this arrogant, vain, small man with a big head? It can only have been that they knew they were in the presence of a *kind* of musical genius without precedent in the history of music, and that to nurture such genius obviated all other considerations. Their faith has been exonerated by the gathering momentum of Wagner's music over the past century, and there is no sign that it will lose that momentum in the future.

The tree-lined road to the Festspielhaus. as painted in 1892 by G. Làska. To this day Wagner's music dramas can be heard each summer in Bayreuth. uncut as the composer intended them. The theater has become the citadel of Wagner performance. a shrine that draws musical pilgrims from around the world

THE WAGNER REPERTORY

STORIES OF THE OPERAS

Compiled by Stephen Wadsworth

DIE FEEN

ACT I.   In a garden in the immortal kingdom of the fairies, two sprites, Farzana and Zemina, call for the separation of Ada, child of a fairy mother and a mortal father, from her mortal lover, Arindal, prince of an earthly realm.

In the wilderness, Gunther and Morald, knights of Arindal's homeland entrusted with finding their sovereign, come upon Gernot, Arindal's servant. Eight years before, Arindal vanished while hunting. Gernot describes how on that distant night Arindal pursued a beautiful doe that eluded him, drawing them forever off the course. Eventually they came to a river, where a voice summoned them to a fabulous castle. Here an exquisite young woman promised herself to Arindal with the proviso that he not question her identity for eight years. They were wed and had two children. Only the previous day, Gernot says, Arindal asked his wife's name and origin and the entire fantasy evaporated. Gunther and Morald go off with Gernot, assuring him that their patron magician, Groma, has instructed them in how to escape the fairies' thrall. The griefstricken Arindal now wanders in to bemoan the loss of his beloved Ada. The knights reappear to relate the sorry state of the homeland to their prince, convincing him to return with

Bust of Richard Wagner
that stands in a flower-filled
glade on the grounds of the
Festspielhaus in Bayreuth

them. Left alone, Arindal is overcome by sleep. The background is transformed into a magic garden, where Ada appears to Arindal and the two assert that their love must withstand all hardship. They are discovered by Arindal's companions and also by Farzana and Zemina, who hail Ada queen of the fairies, bringing news of her father's death. While the fairies rejoice that Ada is now irrevocably fettered to her immortal kingdom, Arindal's friends fear her hold over him. Ada tells Arindal they will meet again, but under dire circumstances: he must swear never to curse her, no matter what horror or evil befall him—he must remain steadfast. The penalty is ruin for them both. Arindal so vows.

ACT II. In the grand foyer of Arindal's ancestral palace, the besieged warriors quake at their seemingly imminent defeat by the enemy. Lora, Arindal's sister and regent of the land since her father's death, reminds her people of Groma's prophecy that the realm will survive if Arindal returns. Everyone is jubilant when a messenger introduces Arindal and his retinue, who prepare for battle. While Morald is reunited with Lora, his fiancée, Gernot enjoys a reunion with his sweetheart, Drolla. When they have followed the others off, Ada materializes with Farzana and Zemina, who mean to force their mistress to renounce Arindal for her immortality. But Ada decides her love will transcend fairy spells and human oaths. The populace returns to await the aid of allies from a neighboring land, and Arindal is confronted by Ada before the assemblage. She conjures up their children and casts them into a fiery pit; the allies arrive and recognize Ada as the woman who led an army down on them, scattering their forces; and there is no hope now for Morald, who is leading the remains of Arindal's troops against an overpowering enemy outside the walls. Undone by her transformation from wife into angel of doom, and by his rampant misfortune, Arindal calls down a curse on Ada. Crushed that he has broken his vow, she explains her behavior is pre-ordained: the fairy king, furious when she fell in love with a mortal, limited her bliss to eight years, after which a series of trials was to be imposed on Ada and Arindal's love. If Arindal stood fast through all adversity, Ada could become mortal; if not she would be turned to stone for one hundred years. Ada now resurrects her children and reveals not only that Arindal's supposed allies were really traitors, but that Morald is on the verge of triumph. As victory is declared, Ada and her underlings vanish into the earth, and the distraught Arindal succumbs to madness.

ACT III. Morald rules the land following Arindal's anguished abdication and descent into dementia. After the court prays intently for Arindal's return to his senses, he himself stumbles in, reliving his meeting with Ada in agonizing hallucinations. Slumbering, he hears her stone-imprisoned voice, then the voice of

Groma, assuring him that he will win Ada back with the help of the shield, sword, and lyre that appear at his feet. Determined to destroy the object of their queen's preoccupying love, Farzana and Zemina waken Arindal and urge him to follow them on a dangerous course to set her free.

They lead him into the underworld, where he is attacked by earth spirits. In the midst of battle, Groma's voice bids Arindal lift his shield at his assailants. They instantly disperse. Encouraged by Groma's spirits, Arindal now faces a phalanx of iron men. This time Groma's voice calls for the sword, with which Arindal drives them off. The astonished Farzana and Zemina, who had expected Arindal to be slain, finally reveal the stone statue of Ada, which, again at Groma's command, Arindal coaxes back to life with the strains of his lyre. Ada's coming to life conjures forth the fairy court. The king rewards Arindal's sincerity and strength with immortality and the fairy throne. The mortals are led in and Arindal bestows his earthly reign on Morald and Lora. Now the lovers, who had alienated their respective kingdoms for love of each other, are reconciled to their peoples and face eternal happiness.

DAS LIEBESVERBOT

ACT I. Sixteenth-century Palermo. Carnival preparations are ruined by the police of Friedrich, Viceroy of Palermo, who has outlawed all forms of pleasure on pain of death. Danieli, Pontio, and Dorella are taken prisoners in their pub; a general demand for an explanation brings about a reading of Friedrich's edict by his Captain of the Watch, Brighella, who is roundly booed by the Sicilians. An example is made of Claudio, who has been condemned to death for being in love. Claudio asks his friend Luzio to beckon his sister, Isabella, from her convent to intervene for him with the Viceroy.

In her retreat, Isabella shares her troubles with Mariana, who reveals that she is Friedrich's wife, abandoned by him for political ambition. Isabella's earnest desire for revenge for the wrongs done herself and Mariana finds the ideal outlet when Luzio arrives with Claudio's news. Isabella will rise to the occasion; Luzio, who has rather fallen for her, will help her rescue Claudio.

At court, Brighella deputizes as judge for Friedrich, who is late, but he gets nowhere with the trial of Danieli, Pontio, and Dorella, whose calculated flirtations disarm him totally. The irate crowd bursts in, followed by Friedrich, who again forbids any festive activity and makes Claudio's sentence law. But Isabella arrives and manages a private meeting with the governor: her beauty capitvates him and he agrees to release Claudio, but her virtue is the price. When she nearly exposes this extortion to the crowd, Friedrich convinces her they wouldn't believe her claim. Instead she remembers Mariana and has an idea that will relieve the tension and free the Sicilians. She makes a rendezvous with Friedrich, apparently agreeing to his terms.

ACT II. Visiting Claudio in prison, Isabella tells of her progress, but his reaction is so dispirited that she leaves him, deploring his cowardice. Alone, she muses on her plan: Mariana will replace her at the rendezvous with Friedrich, who will be notified by letter to come masked to one of the forbidden carnival areas. When she tells Luzio of Friedrich's intentions, he is beside himself and determines to protect her from such humiliation.

In his study, Friedrich is torn between lust and duty: he can no more bring himself to refuse Isabella's charms than to release Claudio honorably. So he signs Claudio's death warrant, but resolves to die after him. Dorella delivers the letter of assignation and makes a rendezvous with Brighella for that evening.

Later, at the end of the Corso, the carnival is gathering joyful force when Brighella turns up with his officers. A near-fight is averted by Luzio, who calms and disperses the merry-makers. Isabella puts the disguised Mariana onto the approaching Friedrich, while Luzio and Brighella both tangle amorously with Dorella. When Pontio brings the intercepted warrant to Isabella and she discovers that Claudio is anything but free, she takes the opportunity to draw the crowd's attention to Friedrich's treachery and disguise. Caught breaking his own law, and secretively with his own wife at that, Friedrich is the object of considerable outrage and derision. But when he asks to be judged by his own law, the fun-loving people show him greater lenience. Claudio is released. Isabella intends to return to the convent to atone for loving Luzio, but when Dorella surrenders Luzio in favor of Brighella, Isabella is delighted to stay among the living. Mariana and Friedrich are reconciled. All celebrate the imminent arrival of the king, and abandon themselves to the carnival fever.

RIENZI

ACT I. Fourteenth-century Rome. On the street before Rienzi's house, a kidnapping attempt by Paolo Orsini and his retainers on Rienzi's sister, Irene, is foiled by members of the Colonna family, Orsini's rivals. The Papal Legate, Raimondo, implores the warring nobles to stop the fighting but is ignored; when Rienzi steps forth to make a patriotic bid for law and order, the nobles also scoff at him and merely put off their brawl until the following morning outside the

Roman walls. But Rienzi has won the support of the gathered citizens, who laud his decision to lock the nobles out of the city until they agree to obey municipal decrees. When the crowd moves on, Rienzi thanks Adriano Colonna for saving Irene and asks if he will join the fight next day. Adriano, inspired by Rienzi's call for Roman solidarity, is also pulled by family loyalty. Rienzi appeals to him to be a citizen first, then departs, leaving Adriano to exchange words of love with Irene.

At daybreak, the people assemble, united under Rienzi, who again speaks for a free Rome. He refuses the city crown, happy as a tribune of the people, unaware that the nobles, closed out and outnumbered, have hatched a plot against him.

ACT II.   In the Capitol, Rienzi's successful guidance of Rome is proclaimed by the people; the realm is clean of strife. At his public address, Rienzi recalls to the nobles the terms of their readmittance into the city. They do not like being reminded of their loss of power, and plan, Orsinis and Colonnas together, to take Rienzi's life. When Adriano overhears this, he begs the nobles to honor Rienzi's deal with them but is rebuffed by one and all. He decides he must save Rienzi. As a festive celebration commences, Adriano warns Rienzi of the conspiracy; as the dancing draws to a close, Orsini sneaks up on Rienzi and tries to stab him, but Rienzi's vest of mail protects him. The people call for the execution of the treasonous plotters—Rienzi so sentences them. But Adriano cannot bear to let his father die, and begs Irene to help him obtain pardon from Rienzi, who is moved to excuse the nobles on condition that they pledge a new allegiance to his cause. While Rienzi's praises are sung, the nobles plan again to undo their adversary.

ACT III.   In the forum, the word is spread that the nobles have mustered an army beyond the city and intend to attack. Rienzi's call to arms inspires an overwhelming response. Adriano laments his conflicting feelings and prays for a sensible reconciliation between the city's new direction and its old patricians. When Rienzi appears clad for battle, Adriano asks if he can act as intermediary to avoid a clash. But Rienzi cannot listen and leads his troops off to battle, leaving Adriano behind with the women, who send up a prayer for their men. Soon Rienzi returns victorious with the bodies of the slain in cortege. Both Orsini and Colonna are dead. Adriano, wild with grief at the death of his father, turns against Rienzi in a rage, but Rienzi brushes him aside.

ACT IV.   Before the Lateran Church, city officials and grudging citizens discuss affairs of state. The nobles have reported to the Pope and the German Emperor that Rome is controlled by a heretic and upstart. Now the Germans have withdrawn their ambassador to Rome. The citizens' uneasiness is encouraged by the bereft Adriano, who determines to murder Rienzi himself but falters when he sees Irene on her brother's arm. As Rienzi enters the church for a service of thanksgiving, however, Raimondo appears to deliver the papal ban on Rienzi. Adriano tells Irene that she too will be excommunicated if she stands by her brother, but she will not abandon Rienzi.

In a room in the Capitol, a stunned Rienzi prays that his followers not desert him. Irene comforts him, refusing to leave him even when he begs her to save herself. Rienzi goes out a last time to try and clear his name. A penitent Adriano meanwhile reiterates the dangers for Irene, but again she turns from him. The angry mob now approaches the Capitol with torches. They will not hear Rienzi's words, though, when he calls to them from a balcony. They stone him and Irene and set fire to the building. When the Capitol crumbles, the wronged knight of Rome and his sister are killed with Adriano, who has tried to rescue them.

DER FLIEGENDE HOLLÄNDER

A Dutch sea captain, Philip Vanderdecken, once swore he would sail around the Cape of Good Hope if it took him forever. The devil held him to his word.

ACT I. Nineteenth century. A violent storm has driven Daland's ship several miles beyond his home on the Norwegian coast. After telling his crew that they have earned a good rest, he leaves the watch in charge of a young steersman, who falls asleep singing a ballad about his sweetheart. As the sky suddenly darkens and the waters again grow rough, a ghostly red-sailed schooner sails into the port and drops anchor next to Daland's ship. Its captain, Vanderdecken, steps ashore, despairing of his fate. Once every seven years he may leave his ship in search of a woman who will redeem him from his deathless wanderings if she gives him faithful, absolute love; failing this, he is condemned to roam until the Day of Judgment. When Daland returns to discover the phantom ship, Vanderdecken tells him of his plight and offers a reward of gold and jewels for a night's lodging. Then, discovering that Daland has a daughter, the Dutchman asks for her hand in marriage. Daland, seeing the extent of the stranger's wealth, immediately agrees and rejoices in his good fortune. Vanderdecken promises his entire treasure cargo as dowry and renews hope for his salvation. The happy Daland, agreeing to meet the Dutchman at his home port, sets sail with the crew, who take up the steersman's song.

ACT II. Daland's young daughter Senta dreamily watches a group of her friends who sit spinning in the family living room under the watchful eye of Mary, her nurse. The girls tease Senta about her suitor, the huntsman Erik, but she remains almost in a trance, staring at a portrait of the Flying Dutchman on the wall. When the superstitious Mary refuses to sing a ballad about the phantom captain, Senta begins the song with burning intensity; to the dismay of her friends, she prays that she may be the one to save the lost man. Erik enters with news of the sailors' return; Mary and the others hurry out to prepare the homecoming feast. The huntsman remains behind and asks the reluctant Senta to plead his case with Daland. Noticing her preoccupation with the Dutchman's picture, he relates a frightening dream in which he saw her passionately embrace the Dutchman and sail away on his ship. Senta exclaims that this is her dream come true, and the despairing Erik rushes away. A moment later, Vanderdecken steps before the girl, who stands transfixed. Daland quickly follows and bids his daughter welcome the stranger, whom he has brought to be her husband. After he leaves, the Dutchman tells of his sad lot, testing Senta's compassion and trust; she ecstatically vows to be faithful to him unto death. Daland comes back and is overjoyed to learn that his daughter has consented to be Vanderdecken's bride.

ACT III. At the harbor, the villagers celebrate the sailors' return with singing and dancing. Perplexed by the strange silence aboard the Dutchman's ship, they invite his men to share the festivities, toasting the neighboring vessel. In answer to the greeting, the ghostly crew derides their captain's quest in hollow chanting; the villagers run away in terror. Senta soon rushes in, pursued by Erik, who insists that she pledged him her love. Vanderdecken overhears the huntsman's claim and brands Senta a faithless woman, bidding his salvation farewell. Senta pleads with him to hear her out, but the Dutchman replies that since she has not yet proclaimed her vows before God, she will escape the eternal damnation of those who betray him. As she replies that she knows his identity and means to save him from his fate, Vanderdecken leaps aboard his vessel just as it sets sail, revealing that he is the Flying Dutchman. While Erik, Mary, and Daland stand transfixed in horror, Senta runs to the edge of the fjord, triumphantly cries that she is faithful unto death, and throws herself into the raging sea. The ghost ship sinks on the horizon as a golden sunrise augurs the transfiguration of Senta and the Dutchman.

TANNHÄUSER

ACT I. Medieval Germany. In the Venusberg, magical mountain abode of

Venus, the minstrel Tannhäuser, deep in thought, kneels beside the flower-laden couch of the goddess, who for more than a year has bestowed her love on him. Fauns and bacchantes chase one another through the rosy mist of the cave, while languorous youths and maidens abandon themselves to the delights of love; the call of sirens echoes from the grottos below. Tannhäuser, who has grown weary of the place, half-heartedly sings a hymn of praise to Venus but ends by imploring his freedom. Surprised, she promises him even greater revels, but the idea only makes him long all the more for the simpler pleasures and pains of earthly life. Enraged, Venus curses his hopes for salvation. He cries out that his hope rests with the Virgin Mary, at whose name the Venusberg disappears.

Tannhäuser finds himself in a sunny valley near the castle of the Wartburg. A young shepherd is singing about spring. As a procession of pilgrims passes enroute to Rome, the minstrel falls to his knees, praising the wonders of God. Soon the sound of horns announces the approach of the Landgrave Hermann and his knights, who are returning from the hunt. When they recognize Tannhäuser, their long-lost comrade, they beg him to accompany them to the castle. One of them, Wolfram, reminds Tannhäuser that in the past his singing won the love of Elisabeth, the Landgrave's beautiful niece. On hearing the girl's name, Tannhäuser embraces his companions and joins them.

ACT II.   In the Hall of Song in the Wartburg, Elisabeth hails the room in which she first heard Tannhäuser's voice. When Wolfram leads in the minstrel, the girl ecstatically welcomes him. When Tannhäuser has gone, Elisabeth and her uncle receive their guests, who enter the hall in stately procession. The Landgrave orders a song contest in praise of love, the winner to claim the hand of Elisabeth. The first of the minstrels to sing, Wolfram delivers an idealized tribute to Elisabeth, whom he too has loved. Tannhäuser, his soul still possessed by Venus, counters this song with a frenzied hymn to the pleasures of worldly love. In dismay, the women rush from the hall as the outraged knights draw their swords to strike the sinner. But Elisabeth, who has remained, throws herself between them to protect Tannhäuser, begging the knights for mercy. At length the Landgrave promises Tannhäuser forgiveness, on the condition that he join a passing band of pilgrims bound for Rome. The remorseful Tannhäuser kisses the hem of Elisabeth's robe, then rushes from the hall to join the pilgrimage.

ACT III.   Several months later, Wolfram discovers Elisabeth at prayer before a shrine in the Wartburg valley, dark with the shadows of an autumn evening. At the approach of a band of pilgrims, she searches among them for Tannhäuser, but in vain. Broken with grief, she prays to the Virgin to receive her soul in heaven. Wolfram, gazing after her as she departs, takes up his harp and asks the evening star to guide her way. As night falls, Tannhäuser staggers in, ragged and weary. He tells Wolfram of his pilgrimage to Rome in abject penitence; of his joy at seeing so many others granted pardon; of his despair when told by the Pope that he could no more be forgiven for his sins than the papal staff break into flower. Reverting to his loyalty to Venus, he summons the goddess, who appears. Wolfram begs the knight not to renounce hope of redemption, bringing him to his senses by invoking the name of Elisabeth. Tannhäuser stands as if transfixed, and at this moment the faithful girl's funeral procession winds down the valley, at which Venus disappears. Supported by Wolfram, Tannhäuser stumbles to Elisabeth's bier, imploring her to pray for him in heaven, and dies. As dawn breaks, a chorus of pilgrims enters singing of a miracle that has taken place: the Pope's staff, which they bear forward, has blossomed.

LOHENGRIN

ACT I. Tenth-century Antwerp. On the banks of the River Scheldt, a herald announces King Henry the Fowler, who has come to raise an army against Hungarian invaders. The king calls on Frederick, Count of Telramund, to explain why the duchy of Brabant is torn by strife and disorder. Telramund charges his ward, Elsa, with the murder of her younger brother Gottfried, heir to the Christian dynasty of Brabant, who disappeared under mysterious circumstances. (Once betrothed to Elsa, Telramund has since married the sorceress Ortrud of Friesland, princess of a pagan rival dynasty.) Summoned to defend herself, Elsa describes a vision in which she beheld a knight in shining armor, who she believes will champion her cause and marry her. Twice the herald calls on the knight to step forward, but only after Elsa has added her own fervent prayer does he appear— on a boat drawn by a swan, whom he bids farewell. The stranger pledges himself to Elsa on the condition that she never ask his name (which is Lohengrin) or origins. She agrees. After the king invokes divine guidance, Lohengrin defeats Telramund in combat to establish the innocence of his bride, with whom he is borne away amid praise and jubilation.

ACT II. Before dawn in the castle courtyard, Telramund reluctantly yields to Ortrud's scheming, hoping to regain favor at court. The two swear vengeance, plotting to undo Lohengrin's credibility and power by firing Elsa's curiosity. No sooner has Elsa appeared on a tower to voice her serenity to the breezes than Ortrud attempts to sow distrust in her mind, calling on pagan gods for help.

Elsa urges the unhappy woman to have faith and offers her friendship, which Ortrud resolves to turn to her own use. They enter the castle as dawn breaks, and the nobles, anticipating the day's events, assemble to hear the Herald proclaim the swan knight guardian of Brabant, while the banned Telramund furtively persuades four treacherous nobles to side with him against the newcomer. The courtiers welcome Elsa as she and her bridal retinue approach in stately procession. At the cathedral entrance, Ortrud attempts to break up the wedding by suggesting that the unknown knight is an impostor, Telramund by accusing him of sorcery. The crowd stirs uneasily. Though Elsa assures her hero she believes in him, the poison of doubt begins to work. The king and his men stand by Lohengrin and the company proceeds into the church.

ACT III. Elsa and Lohengrin, alone in the bridal chamber, have been escorted there by a wedding party singing the praises of love. As the voices die away, the couple express their rapture until anxiety and uncertainty compel Elsa to ask her husband who he is and where he is from. Before the horrified Lohengrin can reply, Telramund and his henchmen burst in. With a cry Elsa hands Lohengrin his sword, with which he kills his assailant. Ordering the nobles to bear Telramund's body to the king, he sadly tells Elsa he will meet her later and answer her questions.

On the banks of the Scheldt, King Henry holds assembly in preparation for the march against the Hungarians. Telramund's bier is brought in, followed by Elsa, scarcely able to walk, and Lohengrin, who declares he cannot now lead the army. Declaring he slew Telramund in self-defense, the knight reveals that his home is the temple of the Holy Grail at distant Monsalvat, where he must now return; Parsifal is his father, Lohengrin his name. Prophesying victory for the king's forces, he bids Elsa farewell and turns to his swan, which has returned for him. Now Ortrud rushes in, exulting in Elsa's betrayal of the man who could have broken the evil spell that caused the disappearance of Gottfried. But Lohengrin's prayers bring Gottfried forth in the place of the vanished swan, and after proclaiming the boy ruler of Brabant, Lohengrin disappears, guided by the dove of the Grail. Ortrud collapses and Elsa, calling for her husband, falls lifeless.

TRISTAN UND ISOLDE

ACT I. The knight Tristan, nephew and successor to King Marke of medieval Cornwall, commands the ship that brings the Irish princess Isolde against her will as bride for Marke. Infuriated by a sailor's song about an Irish girl, Isolde breaks the silence she has maintained since the ship sailed and calls on the elements to sink the ship. Her fury spent, she looks toward Tristan at the helm and muses on his inexplicable betrayal of her. Abruptly she sends her maid, Brangäne, to summon the knight. When Brangäne transmits the command, Tristan's servant, Kurvenal, intervenes with a lusty song of contempt for Isolde and her former fiancé, whom Tristan slew in battle. Brangäne returns, and the humiliated princess tells her how once she cared for a wounded knight, Tantris, only to discover that he was Tristan, the man who had slain her beloved. She tried to kill him, but his plaintive look stopped her; now she curses him, and herself for sparing him. Though Brangäne tries to calm her, the princess chooses a death potion from among magic vials sent with her by her mother. Suddenly, Kurvenal bursts in to tell the women that land has been sighted. Isolde sends him back to Tristan with word that the knight must appear before her now if he hopes to present her to King Marke. She bids the frightened Brangäne farewell, telling her to prepare the death draught. Then Tristan enters. Savagely ridiculing his chivalry, Isolde makes him eager to drink the poison. Tristan, after shouting commands to land the ship, hails the cup as the oblivion for which he longs. He drinks; she wrests the cup from him and drinks as well. The two wait for death. Instead, they rapturously fall into each other's arms, ignoring all the noise of landing and the crew's salute to the king. When Brangäne finally makes them understand that she has substituted a love potion for the poison, they foresee disaster. Tristan leads the fainting Isolde to King Marke.

ACT II.   Outside her apartment in Marke's castle, Isolde and Brangäne listen to the retreating sound of hunting horns. Isolde wants to extinguish the torch, a prearranged signal to Tristan, but Brangäne warns that Marke's night hunting party is a plot by the jealous Melot, Tristan's erstwhile friend, to expose the lovers. Isolde laughs at the girl's accusation and, refusing to wait any longer, gives the signal. Brangäne goes to the watchtower as Tristan appears and rushes into Isolde's arms. Their ardor gives way to an expression of hatred toward the world's rules and obligations (the day) and a glorification of their passion (night). Unnoticed by them, Brangäne floats a warning from the tower. Their desire for ultimate unity makes each ache for death, and their contemplative ecstasy soars until shattered by Brangäne's cry. Kurvenal rushes in, followed by Marke, Melot, and the courtiers. Marke, ignoring Isolde, broken-heartedly asks how his loyal vassal Tristan, who persuaded him to marry Isolde, could have betrayed him. The knight, without answering, asks Isolde to follow him into the land of night, then challenges Melot. But Tristan drops his sword and Melot runs him through.

ACT III.   At his lonely ruined ancestral castle in Brittany, Tristan lies unconscious. The mournful piping of a shepherd, signifying that Isolde's ship is not in sight, wakens the knight. After Kurvenal explains that he has brought him here, Tristan describes how Isolde's face, shining in the hated light of day, drew him back from the blissful night of death. Kurvenal tells him he has summoned Isolde, at which Tristan gives way to a hysterical vision of her arrival. Again hearing the shepherd's tune, he despairs, associating it with a lifelong search for death. Cursing the potion because it was not poison, he collapses, only to revive again with another vision of Isolde. The shepherd sights Isolde's ship and plays a joyful tune. When Kurvenal goes to meet her, Tristan in a frenzy rips off his bandages, hails his blood as his greeting to Isolde, and dies just as she enters. She collapses on his body, not hearing that Marke and Melot are coming. Kurvenal dies fighting Marke's men, but only after he has slain Melot; Marke, who has come to pardon, can only lament. Isolde stirs and, ignoring everyone, describes her vision of the ascent of Tristan's soul. She is transfigured, joining him in night/death.

DIE MEISTERSINGER VON NÜRNBERG

ACT I. Sixteenth-century Nürnberg. As the congregation of St. Katherine's Church sings a closing hymn, the young knight Walther von Stolzing tries to catch the eye of Eva Pogner. After the parishioners have filed out, she informs her suitor that she will be betrothed the next day to the winner of a song contest sponsored by the local guild of Mastersingers. Eva's companion, Magdalene, tells her sweetheart, David, apprentice to the cobbler and poet Hans Sachs, to explain the rules of song composing to Walther, who is taken aback by the complicated ins and outs of mastersinging. David's fellow apprentices set up for a preliminary song trial, and the masters arrive; but before the guild's secretary, Kothner, can call the roll, Walther applies for the contest, making an enemy of fellow contestant Beckmesser, the town clerk—a spiteful, jealous pedant, suspicious of anything new. As proof that tradesmen value art, Pogner offers his daughter's hand as prize for the next day's contest. When Sachs suggests that Eva—and the people—should have some say in the matter, Pogner announces she can reject the winner but must marry a Mastersinger. Now Walther introduces himself, describing his self-taught, natural methods of composition. Going on to his trial song, Walther sings an impulsive, free-form tune, breaking all the Masters' rules, punctuated by Beckmesser's chalk and slate to count the errors. Rejected by the Masters, the young knight stalks out, leaving Sachs to muse on the distinctive appeal of Walther's melody.

ACT II. That evening, as David's fellow apprentices playfully end their day, David tells Magdalene how badly Walther fared. Eva, arriving with her father, gets the sad news from Magdalene. Across the street, Sachs sets up shop in his doorway; the scent of lilacs and the memory of Walther's song, however, distract him. Eva visits him, and though she confesses she would be glad if *he* won the contest, her dismay at his pretended disapproval of Walther betrays her true feelings. Running off in a huff, she is intercepted by Walther, who begs her to elope with him, and they hide while the Night Watchman passes. Sachs lights the street with a lantern, forcing the lovers to stay put while Beckmesser arrives to serenade Eva, whom Magdalene impersonates in Pogner's window. When the clerk is ready with his tune, however, Sachs launches into a lusty song, pleading the need to finish his work. At length they agree that Sachs will drive a nail only when Beckmesser breaks a rule of style. The ensuing racket increases when David jealously attacks the clerk for apparently wooing Magdalene, and the nightshirted neighbors join in a free-for-all until the Watchman's horn disperses them. Pogner leads Eva inside while Sachs drags Walther and David into his shop; in the deserted street the Watchman intones the hour, sounds his horn, and passes through the moonlit, suddenly peaceful street.

ACT III. Reading a book in his study the next morning, Sachs forgives David his unruly behavior and bids him recite his St. John's Day verses. Alone, the cobbler ponders the world's madness, then greets Walther, who tells of a wondrous dream. Sachs recognizes a potential prize song; taking down the words, he helps the knight fashion them, with an ear for form and symmetry. When they depart, Beckmesser limps in and noses around. When he pockets Walther's poem, he is caught by Sachs, who tells him to keep it. Beckmesser, certain of victory, rushes out. Eva now visits Sachs on the pretext of a pinching shoe; Walther returns dressed for the festival and repeats his prize song for her. She is torn between the two men, but the wise older man turns her to the younger. When Magdalene comes in, Sachs promotes David to journeyman with a box on the ear and asks Eva to bless the new song, which all five join in praising. Then they go off to the contest.

In a meadow outside the city, the guilds and citizens assemble under festive banners. After a joyful waltz, the masters file in, Sachs receiving a spontaneous ovation from his people, which in turn inspires a moving address from him. The contest opens as Beckmesser nervously tries to fit Walther's verses to his own music but forgets the words and distorts them, earning laughter from the crowd. The clerk turns furiously on Sachs and scuffles off, missing the rightful delivery of the song by Walther. By this the people are entranced, but Walther refuses the Masters' medallion. Sachs, however, convinces him otherwise, extolling tradition and its upholders as well as its fresh innovators. Youth makes its pact with age, Walther has won Eva, and the people hail Sachs once more as Eva crowns him with Walther's wreath.

DAS RHEINGOLD

Legendary antiquity. In the depths of the Rhine, Woglinde, Flosshilde, and Well-gunde—carefree daughters of the river's spirit—laugh and play. Their song attracts the dwarf Alberich, who tries to catch them. They tease him, luring him on and then escaping, until a golden glow from above lights up the murky waters. The maidens hail this treasure as the Rhinegold and foolishly answer Alberich's questions about it: Woglinde says whoever wins the gold can gain world power, but to do so he must renounce love forever. Since the ugly gnome is getting nowhere with love anyway, he scrambles up the rock and steals the gold. Darkness envelops the scene as he escapes with it, and the Rhinemaidens lament their loss.

High on a mountain, Fricka, goddess of wedlock, wakes her husband Wotan, king of the gods, to show him their newly built castle. He is delighted with it, but Fricka reproaches him for promising her sister Freia, goddess of youth, to the giants Fasolt and Fafner as payment for building the fortress. Suddenly Freia runs in, pursued by the giants; Wotan manages to stall them until further aid arrives with the gods Donner (thunder), Froh (spring), and Loge (fire). The crafty Loge suggests an alternative payment—the ring that Alberich has forged from the Rhinegold, plus the various treasures he has accumulated, in place of Freia. The giants agree, dragging Freia off as hostage until dusk. With the youth goddess gone, the gods begin to age, so Wotan and Loge hurry down through the earth to find Alberich.

In Nibelheim, home of the Nibelung dwarfs, Alberich forces his brother Mime to give him the Tarnhelm, a magic helmet Mime has fashioned which can transform its wearer into any shape or carry him anywhere in a second. Alberich tries it on, vanishes into thin air, and torments Mime before going off to terrorize the other dwarfs. When Wotan and Loge arrive, Mime tells them about Alberich's cruel despotism of Nibelheim. Reappearing with his treasure-bearing subjects, Alberich scatters them with threats and then scoffs at his guests. He plans to conquer the world and enslave the gods. Loge, drawing him out, asks for a demonstration of the Tarnhelm; Alberich obliges, turning himself into a huge serpent, then a tiny toad, which the gods capture easily. Loge snatches the Tarnhelm, and as Alberich resumes his old shape they bind him and drag him off.

Back on the mountain, Alberich is forced to summon his workers to heap up the gold for Freia's ransom. Loge keeps the Tarnhelm—and Wotan wants the ring. Alberich would rather die than give it up, but Wotan wrests it from his finger, suddenly overcome with a lust for its power. The shattered Alberich, freed and powerless, hurls a curse at Wotan: ceaseless worry and death for anyone who wears the ring. After the dwarf has left, the gods assemble with the giants and Freia. Fasolt, who loves Freia, agrees to accept the gold instead only if it completely hides her from his view. Donner, Froh, and Loge pile up the gold and Tarnhelm, but Fasolt can still see her eye through a crack, and Fafner demands the ring to seal it up. Wotan refuses, and the giants start to carry Freia off, stopped only by the materialization of Erda, goddess of the earth. She warns Wotan to surrender the ring, which spells doom for the gods. Taking her advice, Wotan casts the ring on the hoard and immediately witnesses the force of Alberich's curse, as Fafner brutally slays Fasolt in a dispute over it. Lightning and thunder from Donner's hammer clear the air of hovering clouds, and a rainbow appears, forming a bridge to the castle, which Wotan christens Valhalla. As the despairing cries of the Rhinemaidens echo from the valley below, the gods make a stately entrance into their new home.

DIE WALKÜRE

ACT I. As a storm rages, Siegmund the Wälsung, exhausted from pursuit by enemies in the forest, stumbles into an unfamiliar house for shelter. Sieglinde, wife of the house, finds him and the two feel an immediate attraction. But they are soon interrupted by Sieglinde's husband, Hunding, who asks the stranger who he is. Calling himself "Woeful," Sigmund tells of a disaster-filled life, only to learn that Hunding is a kinsman of his foes. Hunding, before retiring, tells his guest to defend himself in the morning. Left alone, Siegmund calls on his father, Wälse, for the sword he once promised him. Sieglinde reappears, having given Hunding a sleeping potion. She tells of her wedding, at which a one-eyed stranger drove into a tree a sword that has resisted every effort to pull it out, then confesses her unhappiness, whereupon Siegmund ardently embraces her and vows to free her from her forced marriage to Hunding. As moonlight floods the room, Siegmund compares their feeling to the marriage of love and spring. Sieglinde hails him as the spring, then asks if his father was really "Wolf," as he said earlier. When Siegmund gives his father's name as Wälse instead, Sieglinde rapturously recognizes him as her twin brother. The Wälsung now draws the sword from the tree and claims Sieglinde as his bride, rejoicing in the union of the blood of the Wälsungs. The two rush off into the spring night.

ACT II. High in the mountains, against a stormy sky, Wotan tells his warrior daughter Brünnhilde she must defend his mortal son Siegmund from Hunding. Leaving joyfully to do his bidding, the Valkyrie pauses to note the approach of Fricka, who storms in to insist that Wotan must defend Hunding's marriage rights against Siegmund, though Wotan argues that Siegmund might save the gods by winning back the Rhinegold before the Nibelung dwarfs regain it. Wotan, caught in his own trap—his power will leave him if he does not enforce the law—agrees to his wife's demands. When Fricka goes in triumph, Wotan tells the returning Brünnhilde about the theft of the gold and Alberich's curse on it. Brünnhilde is shocked to hear her father order her to fight for Hunding. Then, alone in the darkness, she withdraws as Siegmund and Sieglinde approach. Siegmund comforts his distraught sister-bride, who feels herself unworthy of him, and watches over her when she falls asleep. Brünnhilde appears to him as if in a vision, telling him he will soon go to Valhalla, but when he says he will not leave Sieglinde and threatens to kill himself and his bride if his sword has no power against Hunding, she is moved and resolves to help him despite Wotan's command. She vanishes. Siegmund bids farewell to Sieglinde when he hears Hunding's challenge in the distance. In combat, Wotan breaks Siegmund's sword as he is about to win, letting Hunding run him through. Brünnhilde escapes with Sieglinde and the broken sword. Before going after her, Wotan contemptuously fells Hunding with a wave of his hand.

ACT III. When Brünnhilde arrives breathless at the Valkyries' Rock with Sieglinde, her eight warrior sisters are afraid to hide them from the wrathful Wotan. Sieglinde is numb with despair until Brünnhilde tells her she bears Siegmund's child; rapturous and thankful, she accepts the fragments of the sword and flees into the wood. Wotan arrives in a fury to punish Brünnhilde. He sentences her to become a mortal woman, silencing her sisters' laments by threatening to do the same to them. Left alone with her father, Brünnhilde pleads that in disobeying his orders she was really doing what he wished—protecting his favored children. Wotan cannot relent: she must lie in sleep, prize for the man who finds her. But as his anger abates she asks the favor of being surrounded in sleep by a wall of fire that only the bravest hero can pierce. Both sense that this hero must be the child that Sieglinde will bear. Sadly renouncing his daughter, Wotan kisses Brünnhilde's eyes with sleep and mortality before summoning Loge to encircle the rock. As flames spring up, the departing Wotan invokes a spell forbidding the rock to anyone who fears his spear.

SIEGFRIED

ACT I.   Deep in the forest where the dragon Fafner guards the Nibelung treasure and the all-powerful ring, Mime toils at his forge. Greedy, filled with hate but impotent himself, he is at work on yet another sword for his foster son, Siegfried: if the boy can kill the dragon, Mime will get the Nibelung's ring and rule the world. Heralded by a horn call, Siegfried bounds in and teases the terrified Mime with a wild bear. Next he snatches up Mime's latest blade, smashes it, and rages at him for his incompetence. The dwarf calculatingly offers food and kind words, but Siegfried rebuffs him rudely. The youth knows he cannot be Mime's real son, as there is no physical resemblance between them, and he asks who his mother was. Furious at the dwarf's evasions, he grabs him by the throat and demands the truth. For the first time, Mime tells Siegfried about Sieglinde and how she died in childbirth. Siegfried is moved by the story but demands proof—and Mime shows him the fragments of Siegmund's sword, Nothung. Anxious now to see the world, Siegfried orders Mime to repair Nothung and rushes out. As Mime sinks down in despair, the Wanderer (Wotan disguised) enters, weary from his travels, and challenges his host to a battle of wits, the loser to forfeit his head. The stranger easily answers Mime's three riddles—who lives under the earth (the dwarfs), on it (men), and above (the gods)—but Mime gives up in terror when asked who will mend Nothung. The Wanderer departs peacefully, however, leaving Mime's head to the fearless hero who can forge the magic blade. Hearing distant growls, Mime panics, thinking Fafner is coming, but it is Siegfried who enters, ready to wield his father's sword. Mime tries in vain to teach the boy what fear is, and proposes an educational visit to Fafner's lair. Siegfried is all for it and joyfully decides to repair the sword himself. While he works, the dwarf prepares a sleeping potion to give him once he has slain Fafner. Siegfried, flashing the finished sword, splits the anvil and holds up the sword.

ACT II.   That night, in front of Fafner's cave, Alberich broods on the day when the ring will again be his. The Wanderer enters, assuring the startled Nibelung that he is not after the ring, and warns him to watch out for his brother Mime. The Wanderer claims that he is ready to accept what destiny will bring and promises not to interfere—in fact, he advises the sleepy Fafner of Siegfried's intentions. The dragon is not impressed and dozes off again. God and dwarf disappear in the shadows, and as dawn breaks, Mime and Siegfried arrive. The youth dismisses Mime and thinks about his parents, caught up in the peaceful beauty of the woods. Aroused by the song of a forest bird, he tries to imitate it on a homemade reed pipe; he fails and sounds his silver horn instead. This awakens Fafner, who rumbles out of his den and is slain in the ensuing battle. With his dying breath, the dragon warns his killer of the destructive power of the gold. Siegfried accidentally touches a drop of Fafner's blood to his lips, magically enabling him to understand the bird's warblings, which direct him to the treasures in the cave. Now Alberich and Mime appear, quarreling over the spoils, but withdraw as Siegfried comes out with the ring and Tarnhelm. The bird warns him against Mime, who returns with the drugged drink. Reading the dwarf's true thoughts, Siegfried kills him as Alberich's laughter echoes in the distance. The hero is fired by the bird's description of the sleeping Brünnhilde and sets out for new conquests.

ACT III. In a wild mountain pass, the Wanderer summons Erda to learn the gods' fate. She evades his questions, and Wotan resigns himself to Valhalla's doom, bequeathing to the world the redemptive power of Brünnhilde's love. When Siegfried approaches, he angers the god, who attempts to block his path, but with a single stroke of Nothung, Siegfried shatters Wotan's spear and advances.

Dawn breaks on the rocky height where Brünnhilde sleeps. Thinking he has discovered a hero, Siegfried removes her armor and is overcome by her beauty. For the first time he knows what fear is, but he masters his emotions and awakens the maiden with a prolonged kiss. Radiantly hailing the daylight, Brünnhilde rejoices that it is Siegfried who restored her to life. At first she resists his ardor, realizing that earthly love would end her immortal life. But her vanished godhood has made a feeling and vulnerable woman of a chaste Amazon. Bidding Valhalla farewell, she joins Siegfried in praise of love.

GÖTTERDÄMMERUNG

PROLOGUE. On the Valkyries' rock, three Norns spin the rope of fate, recalling Wotan's days of power and predicting Valhalla's fall. When the rope snaps, they descend into the earth in terror to their mother Erda. At dawn Siegfried and his bride Brünnhilde emerge from their cave. Though fearful that she may lose her hero, Brünnhilde sends him forth to deeds of valor. To remind her of his love, Siegfried gives Brünnhilde the magic ring he took from Fafner, taking her horse Grane in exchange. Rapturously they bid farewell as Siegfried sets off on his journey down the Rhine.

ACT I. In their castle on the Rhine, Gunther, king of the Gibichungs, and his sister Gutrune, both unwed, ask counsel of their half brother Hagen. Plotting to secure the ring, Hagen advises Gunther to consolidate his power by marrying Brünnhilde: by means of a magic potion Siegfried can be induced to forget his bride and win her for Gunther in return for Gutrune's hand. The hero's horn announces his approach. Gunther welcomes him, and Gutrune seals his fate by offering him the potion. Hailing Brünnhilde, he drinks and forgets all, quickly succumbing to Gutrune's beauty and agreeing to bring Brünnhilde to Gunther. After solemnizing their bargain with an oath, the men depart. Hagen, keeping watch, gloats on his success.

On the Valkyries' rock, Brünnhilde greets her sister Waltraute, who rushes by to say that Wotan has warned the gods their doom is imminent unless Brünnhilde yields the ring to the Rhinemaidens, but this Brünnhilde refuses to do. Dusk falls as Siegfried reappears disguised as Gunther; wresting the ring from the frightened Brünnhilde, he claims her as Gunther's bride.

ACT II. Before the Gibichung hall, Alberich appears in a dream to his son, Hagen, and forces him to swear he will regain the ring. Siegfried returns as dawn breaks with cheerful greetings for Hagen and Gutrune: he has won Brünnhilde for Gunther, who follows shortly. Hagen summons the vassals to welcome the king and his bride. When Gunther leads in Brünnhilde, she sees Siegfried and recoils; spying the ring on his finger, she decries his treachery and proclaims him her true husband. The hero, still under the potion's spell, vows upon Hagen's spear that he has never wronged her. Brünnhilde swears he lies, but Siegfried dismisses her charge and leaves with Gutrune. The dazed Brünnhilde, bent on revenge, reveals to Hagen the hero's one vulnerable spot: a blade in the back will kill him. Taunted by Brünnhilde and lured by Hagen's description of the ring's power, Gunther joins the murder plot as Siegfried's wedding procession passes by.

ACT III. Near a mossy bank the three Rhinemaidens bewail their lost treasure. Soon Siegfried draws near, separated from his hunting party. The maidens plead for the ring, but he ignores both their entreaties and warnings. When the party arrives, Siegfried at Hagen's urging describes his boyhood with Mime, his slaying of the dragon, and finally—after Hagen gives him another draught to restore his memory—his wooing of Brünnhilde. Pretending indignation, Hagen plunges a spear into the hero's back and walks off. Hailing Brünnhilde with his last breath, Siegfried dies and is borne off.

At the Gibichung hall, Gutrune nervously awaits her bridegroom's return. Hagen tells her Siegfried has been killed by a wild boar, but when his body is carried in she accuses Gunther of murder. Hagen admits the crime. Quarreling over the ring, Gunther is killed by Hagen, who falls back in fear when the dead Siegfried raises his hand. Brünnhilde orders a funeral pyre for Siegfried. Musing on the gods' responsibility for his death, she takes the ring and promises it to the Rhinemaidens. Placing it on her finger, she throws a torch onto the pyre and rides Grane into the flames. As the river overflows its banks and the Gibichung hall is consumed, the Rhinemaidens, dragging Hagen to a watery grave, regain their gold, at last purified of its curse. Flames engulf Valhalla, leaving a human world redeemed by love.

PARSIFAL

ACT I. The Middle Ages. In a forest near the castle of Monsalvat in the Spanish Pyrenees, Gurnemanz, knight of the Holy Grail, rouses his two young esquires from sleep. Two other knights arrive to prepare a morning bath for the ailing monarch Amfortas, who has an incurable wound. They are interrupted by Kundry, an ageless woman of many guises, who rushes in wildly with balsam for Amfortas. The king and his suite now enter, accept the gift, and proceed to the nearby lake. As Gurnemanz bewails Amfortas' wound, his companions ask him to tell about Klingsor, the sorcerer who is trying to destroy them. Gurnemanz explains that Klingsor once tried to join the knightly brotherhood. Denied because of his lustful thoughts, he tried to gain acceptance by castrating himself and was rejected. Now an implacable foe, Klingsor entrapped Amfortas with a beautiful woman; while the king was lying in her arms, Klingsor snatched the Holy Spear and stabbed Amfortas. A prophecy has since revealed that the wound can be healed only by an innocent made wise through compassion. Suddenly a swan falls to the ground, struck by an arrow. The knights drag in a youth, Parsifal, whom Gurnemanz gently rebukes for his foolhardy act. The boy flings away his bow and arrows in shame but cannot explain his conduct or even state his name. Kundry arises to tell the youth's history: his father, Gamuret, died in battle; his mother, Herzeleide, reared the boy in the forest, but now she too is dead. As Kundry falls in a trance, the knights carry Amfortas' litter back from the lake. Gurnemanz leads Parsifal to the castle of the Grail, wondering if the youth enbodies the prophecy's fulfillment.

In the lofty Hall of the Grail, Amfortas and knights prepare to celebrate the Last Supper. The voice of the king's father, the aged Titurel, bids him uncover the holy vessel and proceed, but Amfortas at first hesitates, his anguish rising in the presence of the blood of Christ. At length Titurel orders the esquires to uncover the chalice, which casts its glow about the hall. As the bread and wine are offered, an invisible choir is heard from above. The silent Parsifal understands nothing, but when Amfortas cries out in pain he clutches his heart. Though Gurnemanz angrily drives the uncomprehending boy away, an otherworldly voice reiterates the prophecy.

ACT II. Seated in his dark tower, Klingsor summons his thrall Kundry to seduce Parsifal; having secured the Spear through Amfortas' weakness, he now seeks to inherit the Grail by destroying Parsifal, whom he recognizes as the order's salvation.

In Klingsor's magic garden, Flowermaidens beg for Parsifal's embrace, but when he resists them they disappear. Kundry, transformed into a beautiful siren, woos him with tender memories of his childhood and mother. As she breaks down his resistance and offers a passionate kiss, the boy recoils; at last he understands the mystery of Amfortas' wound and his own mission. Kundry now tries to lure him through pity for the weary life she has been forced to lead ever since she laughed at Christ on the cross, but again she is repulsed. She curses Parsifal to wander hopelessly in search of Monsalvat and calls on Klingsor. The magician hurls the Holy Spear at Parsifal, who catches it in mid-flight and makes the sign of the cross. The castle falls in ruins around him.

ACT III. Gurnemanz, now a hermit and grown old, finds the penitent Kundry exhausted in a thicket near his dwelling. As he revives her, a strange knight in full armor approaches. Gurnemanz recognizes Parsifal and the Holy Spear, whereupon the knight describes his years of trying to find his way back to Amfortas and the Grail. Gurnemanz removes Parsifal's armor; Kundry washes his feet, drying them with her hair. In return he baptizes her, then exclaims at the beauty of the spring fields. The hermit replies that this is the spell of Good Friday. The tolling of distant bells announces the funeral of Titurel. Solemnly they walk toward the castle.

The communion table has vanished from the Hall of the Grail. No longer able to uncover the chalice, Amfortas begs the knights to end his anguish with death. But a new leader, Parsifal, touches Amfortas' breast with the Spear and heals the wound. Raising the sacred chalice aloft, he accepts the homage of the knights as their new king. Kundry, redeemed, falls dying. The brotherhood of the Grail has been saved.

WORLD PREMIERES
AND METROPOLITAN OPERA
PREMIERES

DAS LIEBESVERBOT

Stadttheater, Magdeburg
March 29, 1836
FRIEDRICH: Hr. Gräfe
LUZIO: Hr. Freimuller
CLAUDIO: Hr. Schreiber
ANGELO: Friedrich Krug
BRIGHELLA: Wilhelm Kneisel
ISABELLA: Caroline Pollert
MARIANNE: Fr. Limbach (or Schindler)
DORELLA: Fr. Schindler (or Limbach)
ANTONIO: unknown
DANIELI: unknown
PONTIO PILATO: unknown
CONDUCTED BY Richard Wagner

RIENZI, DER LETZTE DER TRIBUNEN

Königlich Sächsisches Hoftheater, Dresden
October 20, 1842
RIENZI: Josef Tichatscheck
IRENE: Henriette Wüst
ORSINI: Michael Wächter
ADRIANO: Wilhelmine Schröder-Devrient
COLONNA: Georg Wilhelm Dettmer
RAIMONDO: Gioacchino Vestri
BARONCELLI: Friedrich Traugott Reinhold
CECCO: Carl Risse
MESSENGER: Anna Thiele
CONDUCTED BY Richard Wagner

Metropolitan Opera, New York
February 5, 1886 (American Premiere)
RIENZI: Eloi Sylva
IRENE: Lilli Lehmann
ORSINI: Adolf Robinson
ADRIANO: Marianne Brandt
COLONNA: Emil Fischer
RAIMONDO: Phillip Lehmler
BARONCELLI: Otto Kemlitz
CECCO: Emil Sänger
MESSENGER: Ida Klein
CONDUCTED BY Anton Seidl

DER FLIEGENDE HOLLÄNDER

Königlich Sächsisches Hoftheater, Dresden
January 2, 1843
DUTCHMAN: Michael Wächter
SENTA: Wilhelmine Schröder-Devrient
DALAND: Carl Risse
ERIK: Friedrich Traugott Reinhold
MARY: Therese Wächter
STEERSMAN: Wenzel Bielczizky
CONDUCTED BY Richard Wagner

Metropolitan Opera, New York
November 27, 1889
DUTCHMAN: Theodor Reichmann
SENTA: Sophie Weisner
DALAND: Emil Fischer
ERIK: Paul Kalisch
MARY: Charlotte Huhn
STEERSMAN: Albert Mittelhauser
CONDUCTED BY Anton Seidl

TANNHÄUSER

Königlich Sächsisches Hoftheater, Dresden
October 19, 1845
TANNHAUSER: Josef Tichatscheck
VENUS: Wilhelmine Schröder-Devrient
WOLFRAM: Anton Mitterwurzer
ELISABETH: Johanna Wagner
HERMANN: Georg Wilhelm Dettmer
WALTHER: Max Schloss
BITEROLF: Michael Wächter
HEINRICH: Anton Curty
REINMAR: Carl Risse
SHEPHERD: Anna Thiele
CONDUCTED BY Richard Wagner

Salle Le Peletier, Paris
March 13, 1861 (revised)
TANNHAUSER: Albert Niemann
VENUS: Fortunata Tedesco
WOLFRAM: M. Morelli
ELISABETH: Marie Sax
HERMANN: M. Cazaux
WALTHER: M. Aimes
BITEROLF: M. Coulon
HEINRICH: M. König
REINMAR: M. Freret
SHEPHERD: Mlle. Reboux
CONDUCTED BY Pierre Louis-Philippe Dietsch

Metropolitan Opera
November 17, 1884
TANNHAUSER: Anton Schott
VENUS: Anna Slach
WOLFRAM: Adolf Robinson
ELISABETH: Auguste Seidl-Kraus
HERMANN: Josef Kögel
WALTHER: Emil Tiferro
BITEROLF: Joseph Miller
HEINRICH: Otto Kemlitz
REINMAR: Ludwig Wolf
SHEPHERD: Anna Stern
CONDUCTED BY Leopold Damrosch

LOHENGRIN

Hof-Theater, Weimar
August 28, 1850
LOHENGRIN: Carl Beck
ELSA: Rosa Ägthe von Milde
TELRAMUND: Feodor von Milde
ORTRUD: Fr. Fastlinger
HEINRICH: Hr. Höfer
HERALD: August Pätsch
CONDUCTED BY Franz Liszt

Metropolitan Opera, New York
November 7, 1883 (in Italian)
LOHENGRIN: Italo Campanini
ELSA: Christine Nilsson
TELRAMUND: Giuseppe Kaschmann
ORTRUD: Emmy Fursch-Madi
HEINRICH: Franco Novara
HERALD: Ludovico Cantini
CONDUCTED BY Auguste Vianesi

TRISTAN UND ISOLDE

Königlich Hof- und National-Theater, Munich
June 10, 1865
TRISTAN: Ludwig Schnorr von Carolsfeld
ISOLDE: Malvina Schnorr von Carolsfeld
KURVENAL: Anton Mitterwurzer
BRANGANE: Anna Possart-Deinet
MARKE: Ludwig Zottmayer
MELOT: Karl Samuel Heinrich
SHEPHERD: Karl Simons
SAILOR'S VOICE: unknown
STEERSMAN: Peter (or Adolf) Hartmann
CONDUCTED BY Hans von Bülow

Metropolitan Opera, New York
December 1, 1886 (American Premiere)
TRISTAN: Albert Niemann
ISOLDE: Lilli Lehmann
KURVENAL: Adolf Robinson
BRANGANE: Marianne Brandt
MARKE: Emil Fischer
MELOT: Rudolph von Milde
SHEPHERD: Otto Kemlitz
SAILOR'S VOICE: Max Alvary
STEERSMAN: Emil Sänger
CONDUCTED BY Anton Seidl

DIE MEISTERSINGER VON NÜRNBERG

Königlich Hof- und National-Theater, Munich
June 21, 1868
HANS SACHS: Franz Betz
EVA: Mathilde Mallinger
WALTHER: Franz Nachbaur
MAGDALENE: Sophie Diez
DAVID: Max Schlosser
POGNER: Kaspar Bausewein
BECKMESSER: Gustav Hölzel
KOTHNER: Karl Fischer
VOGELGESANG: Karl Samuel Heinrich
NACHTIGALL: Eduard Sigl
ZORN: Bartholomäus Weixlstorfer
EISSLINGER: Eduard Hoppe
MOSER: Michael Pöppl
ORTEL: Franz Thoms
SCHWARTZ: Leopold Grasser
FOLTZ: Ludwig Hayn
WATCHMAN: Ferdinand Lang
CONDUCTED BY Hans von Bülow

Metropolitan Opera, New York
January 4, 1886 (American Premiere)
HANS SACHS: Emil Fischer
EVA: Auguste Seidl-Kraus
WALTHER: Albert Stritt
MAGDALENE: Marianne Brandt
DAVID: Felix Krämer
POGNER: Josef Staudigl
BECKMESSER: Otto Kemlitz
KOTHNER: Phillip Lehmler
VOGELGESANG: Hr. Dworsky
NACHTIGALL: Emil Sänger
ZORN: Hr. Hoppe
EISSLINGER: Hr. Klaus
MOSER: Hr. Langer
ORTEL: Max Dörfler
SCHWARTZ: Hermann Weber
FOLTZ: Hr. Anlauf
WATCHMAN: Carl Kaufmann
CONDUCTED BY Anton Seidl

DAS RHEINGOLD

Königlich Hof- und National-Theater, Munich
September 22, 1869
WOTAN: August Kindermann
FRICKA: Sophie Stehle
LOGE: Heinrich Vogl
FROH: Franz Nachbaur
DONNER: Karl Samuel Heinrich
FREIA: Henriette Müller
ERDA: Emma Seehofer
ALBERICH: Emil Fischer
MIME: Max Schlosser
FAFNER: Kaspar Bausewein
FASOLT: Toni Petzer
WOGLINDE: Anna Kaufmann
FLOSSHILDE: Wilhelmine Ritter
WELLGUNDE: Therese Vogl
CONDUCTED BY Franz Wüllner

Metropolitan Opera, New York
January 4, 1889 (American Premiere)
WOTAN: Emil Fischer
FRICKA: Fanny Moran-Olden
LOGE: Max Alvary
FROH: Albert Mittelhauser
DONNER: Alois Grienauer
FREIA: Katherine Senger-Bettaque
ERDA: Hedwig Reil
ALBERICH: Joseph Beck
MIME: Wilhelm Sedlmayer
FAFNER: Eugene Weiss
FASOLT: Ludwig Mödlinger
WOGLINDE: Sophie Traubmann
FLOSSHILDE: Hedwig Reil
WELLGUNDE: Felicie Kaschowska
CONDUCTED BY Anton Seidl

DIE WALKÜRE

Königlich Hof- und National-Theater, Munich
June 26, 1870
SIEGMUND: Heinrich Vogl
SIEGLINDE: Therese Vogl
HUNDING: Kaspar Bausewein
BRUNNHILDE: Sophie Stehle
WOTAN: August Kindermann
FRICKA: Anna Kaufmann
GERHILDE: Karoline Leonoff
ORTLINDE: Henriette Müller
WALTRAUTE: Fr. Hemauer
SCHWERTLEITE: Emma (Therese?) Seehofer
HELMWIGE: Anna Possart-Deinet
SIEGRUNE: Walburga (Anna?) Eichheim
GRIMGERDE: Wilhelmine Ritter
ROSSWEISSE: Juliane Tyroler
CONDUCTED BY Franz Wüllner

Metropolitan Opera, New York
January 30, 1885
SIEGMUND: Anton Schott
SIEGLINDE: Auguste Seidl-Kraus
HUNDING: Josef Kögel
BRUNNHILDE: Amalie Friedrich-Materna
WOTAN: Josef Staudigl
FRICKA: Marianne Brandt
GERHILDE: Marianne Brandt
ORTLINDE: Anna Stern
WALTRAUTE: Anna Gutjar
SCHWERTLEITE: Carrie Morse
HELMWIGE: Anna Robinson
SIEGRUNE: Anna Slach
GRIMGERDE: Fr. Kemlitz
ROSSWEISSE: Helena Brandl
CONDUCTED BY Leopold Damrosch

SIEGFRIED

Festspielhaus, Bayreuth
August 16, 1876
SIEGFRIED: Georg Unger
BRUNNHILDE: Amalie Friedrich-Materna
WANDERER: Franz Betz
ERDA: Luise Jaïde
MIME: Carl Schlosser
ALBERICH: Karl Hill
FAFNER: Franz von Reichenberg
FOREST BIRD: Lilli Lehmann
CONDUCTED BY Hans Richter

Metropolitan Opera, New York
November 9, 1887 (American Premiere)
SIEGFRIED: Max Alvary
BRUNNHILDE: Lilli Lehmann
WANDERER: Emil Fischer
ERDA: Marianne Brandt
MIME: T. Ferenczy
ALBERICH: Rudolph von Milde
FAFNER: Johannes Elmblad
FOREST BIRD: Auguste Seidl-Kraus
CONDUCTED BY Anton Seidl

GÖTTERDÄMMERUNG

Festspielhaus, Bayreuth
August 17, 1876
SIEGFRIED: Georg Unger
BRUNNHILDE: Amalie Friedrich-Materna
WALTRAUTE: Luise Jaïde
GUNTHER: Eugen Gura
GUTRUNE: Mathilde Weckerlin
HAGEN: Gustav Siehr
ALBERICH: Karl Hill
FIRST NORN: Johanna Wagner
SECOND NORN: Josephine Scheffsky
THIRD NORN: Friederike Grün
WOGLINDE: Lilli Lehmann
FLOSSHILDE: Marie Lehmann
WELLGUNDE: Minna Lammert
CONDUCTED BY Hans Richter

Metropolitan Opera, New York
January 25, 1888 (American Premiere)
SIEGFRIED: Albert Niemann
BRUNNHILDE: Lilli Lehmann
WALTRAUTE: role cut
GUNTHER: Adolf Robinson
GUTRUNE: Auguste Seidl-Kraus
HAGEN: Emil Fischer
ALBERICH: Rudolph von Milde
FIRST NORN: role cut
SECOND NORN: role cut
THIRD NORN: role cut
WOGLINDE: Sophie Traubmann
FLOSSHILDE: Marianne Brandt
WELLGUNDE: Louise Meisslinger
CONDUCTED BY Anton Seidl

PARSIFAL

Festspielhaus, Bayreuth *July 22, 1882*	Metropolitan Opera, New York *December 24, 1903* (American Premiere)
PARSIFAL: Hermann Winkelmann	PARSIFAL: Alois Burgstaller
KUNDRY: Amalie Friedrich-Materna	KUNDRY: Milka Ternina
AMFORTAS: Theodor Reichmann	AMFORTAS: Anton Van Rooy
GURNEMANZ: Emil Scaria	GURNEMANZ: Robert Blass
TITUREL: August Kindermann	TITUREL: Marcel Journet
VOICE: Sophie Dompierre	VOICE: Louise Homer
FIRST ESQUIRE: Hermine Galfy	FIRST ESQUIRE: Katherine Moran
SECOND ESQUIRE: Mathilde Keil	SECOND ESQUIRE: Paula Braendle
THIRD ESQUIRE: Max Mikorey	THIRD ESQUIRE: Albert Reiss
FOURTH ESQUIRE: Adolf von Hübbenet	FOURTH ESQUIRE: Willy Harden
FIRST GRAIL KNIGHT: Anton Fuchs	FIRST GRAIL KNIGHT: Julius Bayer
SECOND GRAIL KNIGHT: Eugen Stumpf	SECOND GRAIL KNIGHT: Adolph Mühlmann
KLINGSOR: Karl Hill	KLINGSOR: Otto Goritz
FIRST MAIDEN: Pauline Horson	FIRST MAIDEN: Katherine Moran
SECOND MAIDEN: Johanna Meta	SECOND MAIDEN: Lillian Heidelbach
THIRD MAIDEN: Carrie Pringle	THIRD MAIDEN: Fr. Försen
FOURTH MAIDEN: Johanna André	FOURTH MAIDEN: Paula Braendle
FIFTH MAIDEN: Hermine Galfy	FIFTH MAIDEN: Florence Mulford
SIXTH MAIDEN: Luise Belce	SIXTH MAIDEN: Isabelle Bouton
CONDUCTED BY Hermann Levi	CONDUCTED BY Alfred Hertz

DIE FEEN

Königlich Hof- und National-Theater, Munich
June 29, 1888

FAIRY KING: Victorine Blank
ADA: Lili Dressler
ZEMINA: Pauline Sigler (Siegler)
FARZANA: Marie (Margarethe) Sigler (Siegler)
ARINDAL: Max Mikorey
GUNTHER: Heinrich Herrmann
MORALD: Rudolf Fuchs
GERNOT: Gustav Siehr
LORA: Adrienne Weitz
DROLLA: Emilie Herzog
HARALD: Kaspar Bausewein
MESSENGER: Max Schlosser
CONDUCTED BY Franz Fischer

INDEX

Page numbers in italics indicate captioned material

180